The present generation of mankind is the first one that can irreversibly transform our planet for the worse. It is also the last generation with the capacity to introduce the changes required to avert environmental disaster. South Africa is a microcosm of the challenges facing the world. Will we choose a path which provides a rich and sustainable heritage for our children or will we descend into a wasteland of lost opportunities?

This book describes both global and regional trends in environmental health, from the potential holocaust of a 'nuclear winter' to the insidious, invisible threat of the 'greenhouse effect' and the ozone hole. Against this background of global change, the South African environmental 'rules of the game' are analysed. These include the country's immense biotic diversity, its weather cycles, human population dynamics, mass urbanization, water and energy resources, commercial agricultural wealth and homeland poverty, marine resources and consumer spending patterns.

Two 'key uncertainties' – the different socioeconomic paths and environmental management ethics that South Africa might adopt – are used to derive four possible environmental scenarios in the early 21st century. They range from the 'Paradise Lost' of a regional wasteland and the 'Separate Impoverishment' of continuing down the 'Low Road', to the 'High Road' options of 'Boom and Bust' where our natural resources are plundered to achieve maximum short-term economic gains and 'Rich Heritage' where sustained development is pursued.

This book is unique in its integration of political, social, economic and environmental issues. Its roots lie in an all-embracing philosophy of nature. The book provides a fresh look at South Africa's choices for the future – a future which South Africans alone can determine.

Brian Huntley, Roy Siegfried
and Clem Sunter

South African Environments into the 21st Century

HUMAN & ROUSSEAU

TAFELBERG

First published in 1989 jointly by
Human & Rousseau (Pty) Ltd, State House, 3-9 Rose Street, Cape Town
and Tafelberg Publishers Ltd, 28 Wale Street, Cape Town
Set in 10.5 on 13 pt Plantin by Diatype Setting, Cape Town
Printed and bound by National Book Printers, Goodwood, Cape
First edition 1989, third impression 1990

ISBN 0 624 02658 2

FOR MERLE, RONA
AND MARGARET

Contents

Preface

Early in 1988, Rick Lomba, a producer of wildlife films, visited me at Anglo American Corporation and dropped off a video he had made called 'The End of Eden'. It dealt with the adverse impact of cattle ranching on the environment in Botswana. It shook me that in all the research which Anglo's global and South African scenario teams had done, we had paid scant attention to the environment.

Rick introduced me to Brian Huntley of the Council for Scientific and Industrial Research (CSIR) and Roy Siegfried of the University of Cape Town, both of whom are eminent in environmental affairs. They had been keen for some time to undertake a general study of the future South African environment. In particular, they were sceptical as to whether the 'High Road' scenario for South Africa could be achieved without excessive environmental cost. It was a challenge to prove the exact opposite: the 'High Road' as a precondition for a sound environment.

I agreed to join Brian and Roy in the research programme and Anglo agreed to support it. We held two workshops later in 1988. Included in these workshops were Jock Danckwerts, Dave Dewar, George Ellis, Symond Fiske, Tim Hart, Fred Kruger, Mike Mentis, Elize Moody, Graham Noble, John Raimondo, Roland Schulze, Butch Smuts, Rob Soutter and Jenny Thomson.

What the workshops exposed was a wide variety of opinion not only on environmental issues but also on political, economic and social questions. It became apparent that the study could not be confined solely to the environment. It had to take into account the other issues, as they are all interrelated with one another and with the environment.

We decided not to re-invent the wheel. Instead, we used the 'High Road', 'Low Road' and 'Wasteland' material that had already been put together by the Anglo scenario team. Then we superimposed the environmental options onto these socioeconomic trajectories.

The result was a presentation entitled 'South African Environments into the 21st Century' which we gave to Anglo's Executive Committee at the beginning of March 1989. They have allowed us to publish this material, in the same way that I was previously allowed to publish the book *The World and South Africa in the 1990s*. Similarly, this book repesents the views of the team which finally put the study together, namely the three of us. We were given total discretion over the material. It does not reflect a 'corporate viewpoint'.

We would like to thank Anglo for its support of this project. We also wish to express our appreciation for the invaluable contributions made in the two workshops by the participants, without which this book would not have been possible. Special mention must be made of Merle Huntley, Brian's wife, who did an enormous amount of work on the manuscript, and of Diana Banyard who undertook, in a most efficient manner, the typing of the manuscript and the administration of the project. Of course, we are indebted to Rick Lomba for bringing us together in the first place.

Lastly, I must thank my two colleagues, Brian and Roy, for the intellectual stimulation and sheer fun I have had in assisting them to write this book. It was a real privilege. I wish to end with a quotation from Brian which provides a good justification for all the work we have done.

"On 14 November 1974, while undertaking an aerial survey of Cameia National Park in central Angola, I made an unscheduled landing alongside the Benguela railway, just east of Jonas Savimbi's home town. After a long wait, an armed troop train approached and stopped. I joined a motley garrison of Portuguese soldiers retiring from the border post of Teixeira da Sousa adjoining Zaïre. The garrison had been routed the previous day. They described the sad state of affairs across the border in Dilolo, a ghost town of decaying buildings, potholed roads, empty shops and starving children. But that was Zaïre, they said — Angola would never go that way. It was too rich, its people too committed, its infrastructure too strong.

On 19 August 1975, I passed through the deserted, burnt-out villages of Humbe and Fort Rocadas near Angola's border with Namibia, as I moved southwards with a column of 10 000 refugees. We left the magnificent country, no less strong than South Africa, to the ravages of civil war and a downward spiral towards a regional wasteland."

CLEM SUNTER

1 Beyond Greenpeace

This book is about our future wellbeing in South Africa. It is designed to make South Africans aware of their environment. It demonstrates that neither limitations of resources nor burgeoning human numbers need be constraints on development in the foreseeable future. South Africans have the potential to reach a high quality of life across the board early in the 21st century. In pursuit of this goal, the meaningful participation of all who live here may prove to be the most formidable obstacle to political revolution and to the creation of an environmental wasteland.

Nevertheless, the book confronts South Africans with tough choices which will have long-term environmental consequences – for us, our children and our grandchildren. Hardest of all, the decisions must be taken now, albeit sometimes on soft evidence. We cannot wait for another generation.

The book is not an impassioned treatise on environmental morality, the sole purpose of which is to deplore the sad plight of the African elephant or the imminent extinction of the golden gladiolus. Neither is it one of those studies put together by a committee of environmentalists who, in seeking not to be controversial, end up with a string of motherhood statements and a tedious inventory of natural resources.

No, this book is about the realities facing one species, *Homo sapiens*. Can we keep the options open for future generations so that they have a wider choice of ideas, life styles and environments than we have today?

After all, it is that widening choice which characterizes the progress of civilization and distinguishes us from our cave-dwelling ancestors. On the one hand, the human race can survive under conditions of great physical and psychological deprivation. On the other, civilization cannot flourish unless people have access to natural resources and a healthy environment, deriving material and spiritual benefit from both of them.

An April 1989 edition of *Time* carried an article lamenting the lack

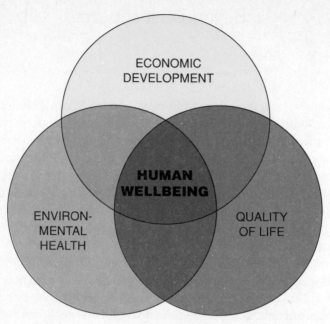

Chart 1 · The three determinants of human wellbeing

of time in America for reflection, creativity and leisure. According to one survey, the amount of leisure time enjoyed by the average US citizen has fallen by 37% since 1973, the opposite of the trend predicted from technological advances. Add to this the loss of species, the shrinking of unspoilt wilderness and an ever rising cost of living, and perhaps the current generation of young Americans will be the first in history to have less freedom of choice than their parents.

The prime objective of most nations has been the growth in production of goods and services. It still is. However, the central thesis of this book is that human wellbeing depends on a favourable interaction between economic development, environmental health and quality of life.

The first two dimensions are obvious. Economic development provides the individual with shelter, food, clothing, the basic material necessities and the luxuries of life. Environmental health is manifest in a beautiful countryside, clean rivers and lakes, pristine beaches, land that remains bountiful for centuries and towns that are well laid out and free of pollution. Quality of life is a more elusive and abstract concept. It is difficult to measure because it is highly subjective. It has to do with faith, freedom of the spirit, happiness and self-fulfilment. It goes along with a sound political structure.

All three dimensions are necessary for a fulfilled life.

In the South African context, the ideal of sustained development – meaning development which ensures that the use of resources and the environment today does not damage prospects for future generations – can only be approached through a path of sustained economic growth. For without this, there can be little improvement in the condition of the environment and the quality of human life.

Even on such a path, however, economic growth, the state of the environment and the quality of life cannot be maximized simultaneously and equally. South Africa, in common with other countries, will have to develop its own dynamic model and make its own trade-offs. In doing so, South African commerce and industry will have to examine opportunities for new economic ventures within the framework of this question: how can societies meet basic human needs and nurture economic growth without undermining the natural resources and environmental integrity on which life, economic vitality and national security depend?

In the 1950s and 1960s, industrial production soared in many parts of the world, including South Africa. This triggered a backlash in the 1960s and 1970s, primarily among young people around the world who rebelled against the emphasis placed on military might and the accumulation of wealth as measures of success. Out of this concern was born the 'hippie' movement, 'flower power' and the caustic lyrics of Bob Dylan. The environmental cause, so long a lonely crusade of natural scientists, was taken up by people who were anti-Establishment and anticapitalist. This later crystallized into political movements such as the 'Greens' in Western Europe.

In contrast, however, the late 1980s have witnessed a more sober review of the state of the global environment – but one which has placed environmental issues on the agenda of the superpowers and the other major industrialized nations. (An environmental issue even led to the resignation of the Dutch government in May 1989: members of the ruling coalition could not agree on who should pay for a plan to cut pollution by 70% in the Netherlands by 2010.) All this implies that the growing linkage between human development and environmental health will be a dominant force in global affairs in the 21st century, possibly replacing military and economic power play as the focus of international concern. This change in perception is due to a growing understanding among nations of six important points:

- Environmental problems, such as air and water pollution and human numbers, are no longer only of local or regional importance but have global implications.
- Serious risks to the environment, previously detected because they were acute or conspicuous, may now arise insidiously and can even be invisible. Headline grabbers such as the oil spill in Alaska or the nuclear power accident at Chernobyl do not pose an overall threat to mankind. The growth in fossil fuel consumption does.
- Episodes of apparently short-term, reversible environmental damage might affect not only the present generation, but also future ones because of the momentum already built into the ecological system.
- Sustained economic development is a fundamental prerequisite for the maintenance of a healthy global environment and vice versa.
- Utopian social engineering stands little chance of success, as demonstrated in mainland China, the USSR and Africa. The state of the environment and the degree of environmental awareness in China and the USSR are appalling, to say the least. As one wag put it, socialism is the long, hard road between capitalism and capitalism.
- Individual rights and freedoms, underpinned by common law, private ownership of resources and a free-market economy, go hand in hand with sustained economic development.

The last two points show where the 'Greens' have gone wrong. They contradict themselves by demanding socialism and a clean environment at the same time. Socialism leads inevitably to the malfunctioning of the economy, which means that no money is available for conservation. Perhaps modern psychologists who believe that the human mind thinks most efficiently in a survival mode have the answer. Man is a born opportunist. By denying that self-interest is a valid principle, socialists are suppressing people's innate ability to think in an efficient

NEW PERCEPTIONS OF THE GLOBAL ENVIRONMENT

- **Environmental problems have global implications**
- **Serious risks arise insidiously and may be invisible**
- **Apparently reversible impacts could affect future generations**

Chart 2

manner. The student uprising in China, the election victory of Solidarity in Poland and the re-emerging nationalisms of the people of the Soviet Union serve to confirm that communism is an unnatural philosophy inflicted on mankind. We could be in for turbulent times in the communist world.

Much of the available global evidence points to a wasteland scenario within the next century worse than the most negative predictions of the environmental lobby of the 1960s. Yet all is not gloom and doom. While the present generation of mankind is the first to have the power drastically and irreversibly to transform the planet for the worse, it is also the only generation capable of preventing such an evolution. Exciting opportunities are emerging for the imaginative use of new technologies which avoid pollution or which clean up environmental damage. Modern technology, once the greatest foe of many environmentalists, may yet become their most valued ally.

Many environmentalists have an abiding obsession: to formulate recommendations on how to right the world's wrongs. Our study presents no recommendations or prescriptions. However, it covers much wider ground than a plain environmental exercise, because the environment is intertwined with politics and economics. It describes a few of many possible futures for South Africa, with indications of their environmental consequences and some general conclusions. We leave the choices to the reader. The only certainty is that the time for making choices is running out. Within the next decade, the option for creating a prosperous South Africa will be foreclosed, and with it will go all the promise of one of the world's most generously endowed regions.

2 Structure of the Book

The approach taken to look at the future environment is similar to that used in Clem Sunter's *The World and South Africa in the 1990s*, published in May 1987 by the publishers of this book. It is based on the technique of scenario planning, whereby the future is depicted as a broad range of possibilities, not pinpointed as a sharply defined forecast.

We do not like forecasts, even when there is a consensus among experts. This is nowhere better illustrated than in the oil industry in which, to quote an experienced source, "a group of oil price forecasters make a flock of sheep look like independent thinkers". The scenario planning technique is, moreover, peculiarly well suited to the subject in hand because it integrates all the factors which could have a bearing on the environment – political, economic and ecological.

In this book, we first set the scene by describing some of the alarm bells which are beginning to ring in regard to the world environment. The information presented is drawn from a continuing international research programme on global change. Many of the trends alluded to in the text have been hotly debated and subjected to exhaustive review.

THE STRUCTURE OF THE BOOK

* **Introduction: Beyond Greenpeace**
* **Future environments of Planet Earth: global alarm bells**
* **The South African environment in the 1980s**
* **Environmental 'rules of the game'**
* **'Key uncertainties'**
* **South African environmental scenarios**
* **Conclusions**

Chart 3

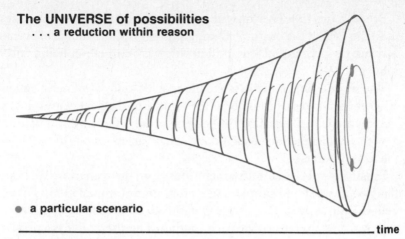

The UNIVERSE of possibilities
. . . a reduction within reason

● a particular scenario

time

Chart 4 · The cone of uncertainty

Now, however, they are widely accepted by leading authorities in the relevant scientific fields.

We then consider the South African* environment in the 1980s, in particular the tremendous impact that climate and weather have had on ecosystems made vulnerable through a century or more of use and abuse. This catalogue of dramatic events is a suitable prelude to laying down South Africa's environmental 'rules of the game', which include its basic geography, variability of climate, agricultural potential, distribution of resources and human settlement patterns. These and other factors, which are common to all possible futures, narrow the 'cone of uncertainty' that opens out as one gazes into the future.

The next step is to identify 'key uncertainties'. As the name implies, these are events or courses of action which can propel the future into quite different directions. The interaction of the latter – within the boundaries set by the 'rules of the game' – provides a suite of scenarios for South Africa's future environment. (A scenario is merely a plausible story about the future, illustrating one of several possibilities.)

*The terms 'South Africa' or 'South African' refer to the Republic of South Africa together with the self-governing states falling within it, such as KwaZulu, and the Republics of Transkei, Bophuthatswana, Venda and Ciskei (the TBVC). The term 'homelands' denotes the TBVC and self-governing states. Unless otherwise stated, statistics relate to South Africa as defined above.

17

Broadly, two time horizons can be discerned in this study. One takes us to the turn of the century. During this period, the course of events is relatively predetermined and known, the information being fairly robust.

The second time horizon is the life span of today's youngest generation, which takes us roughly to the middle of the next century. Any statement made concerning this longer period is far more speculative, as even a modest action taken today can have an enormous impact over the next 60 years.

Finally, we derive certain conclusions from the scenarios. We hope that people will build simple action programmes around them. For we believe in an active future – one that is made to happen by South Africans working in concert with one another. The alternative is a passive future, where society, through negligence, allows the options to be closed and the future to be imposed on it. With this book, we want to alert South Africans to the options currently available, and to encourage them to participate actively in creating a better environment. Nothing more. Nothing less.

3 Future Environments of Planet Earth

As the first step in developing scenarios, we sought an overall perspective of our changing planet.

Among many trends and possibilities, we perceived four that could most strongly influence the environments of the 21st century. The first of these, world population growth, is already a familiar concern. The second and third, global warming and depletion of the ozone layer, have only recently been recognized as of more than academic interest. These three processes have developed a momentum which at best can be slowed. At worst and if not controlled, they could in combination lead to a long-term erosion of the quality of life of all people, the onset of mass extinctions of plant and animal species, and the irreversible pollution of land and ocean with toxic waste. The disappearance of civilizations developed over the past 5 000 years would follow.

The fourth, and most dramatic possibility in the short term, is nuclear war. Though the least probable, it cannot be ruled out. Let us deal with it first.

A SUDDEN 'NUCLEAR WINTER'

While the human population explosion and global warming have consequences measured in decades, a major nuclear war could totally transform the planet and annihilate plant and animal life over vast areas within a few weeks or months. This worst-case scenario, popularly termed the 'nuclear winter', has moved from the pages of science fiction to become a chillingly real threat.

What is the 'nuclear winter'? In 1980, scientists suggested that the mass extinction of species that occurred 65 million years ago could be attributed to the blocking out of sunlight by a dust cloud. The cloud was thrown into the atmosphere by a massive asteroid striking the earth. A cloud of equally dramatic proportions would be created from the firestorms generated by a major nuclear war. It was this concept which stimulated a global study of the environmental effects of nuclear war. The study, known as ENUWAR, involved over 300 scien-

POSSIBLE CHANGES TO PLANET EARTH

✻ 'Nuclear winter'
✻ Population growth
✻ Global warming
✻ The 'ozone hole'

Chart 5

tists from 30 countries and was led by Sir Frederick Warner of the University of Essex. It was completed in 1987.

Various nuclear war scenarios were developed by the ENUWAR team. The most plausible intimated that an intercontinental confrontation would release 6 000 megatonnes – about half the arsenal available to the USA and USSR. This is 2 000 times the total fire power used in the Second World War – a mere three megatonnes. The enormous destructive power of today's military machine is illustrated by the new Trident submarine. At 24 megatonnes, its fire power is enough to destroy all the major cities in the northern hemisphere!

The study concluded that the dense smoke clouds resulting from a nuclear war in which 6 000 megatonnes of warheads were detonated in the northern hemisphere would reduce the sunlight reaching the ground by 90%. The clouds would spread rapidly around the globe, over both northern and southern hemispheres. This would cause a drop of 15-20 °C in mean daily temperatures for several weeks: hence the term 'nuclear winter'.

The immediate and direct impact of the war would be between 100 million and 1 000 million deaths. Furthermore, the majority of the world's remaining population would face starvation in the war's aftermath owing to the disruption of agriculture, transport and food aid. Even nations of the southern hemisphere not involved in the war would suffer severe losses. It could mean between 100 million and 450 million people running out of food in Africa within the first 10 days of a war in which not a single nuclear weapon struck the continent.

South Africa could be the least affected country in Africa, but the destruction of trade, and of cultural and scientific links with the rest of the world, would have adverse consequences for our quality of life. Radiation sickness and the multitude of other effects of a major nuclear war would leave few survivors. In a tragically ironic twist, fate would grant these survivors little more than a brief reprieve – just long enough for them to envy the dead.

At a time in which the combined USA/USSR strategic nuclear arsenals have the potential to release a Hiroshima-scale detonation every second for nearly 12 days – one million Hiroshimas – a 'nuclear winter' is a wild card that cannot be ignored in the pack of environmental driving forces. The widely acclaimed Intermediate-range Nuclear Forces (INF) Treaty covers a mere 4% of the weaponry available to the superpowers: cold comfort for those who would prefer to leave the hypothesis of 'nuclear winter' untested.

On the positive side, reductions may be made in the near future in the numbers of intercontinental ballistic missiles held by the two superpowers. Nevertheless, a greater possibility now exists of a nuclear strike by one Third World country against another. Alternatively, a city may be held to ransom by terrorists who have managed to gain possession of a nuclear device. Though smaller in scale, such events could trigger a wider conflict.

But, more worrying than either of these threats is a nuclear war accidentally started through misunderstanding, mistrust or technical malfunction. A recent study of the Cuban missile crisis of 1962 revealed the apalling ignorance of both superpowers to the other's real position during the affair. They came to within a hair's breadth of war.

THE ALL-PERVASIVE IMPACT OF POPULATION GROWTH

Many environmental futurists predict, like T. S. Eliot, that the world will not go out with a bang, but with a whimper – pulled relentlessly into the pit of starvation by the weight of human numbers.

It is now 20 years since Paul Ehrlich wrote *The Population Bomb*, which focused world attention on the environmental consequences of too many humans. Subsequent studies, such as the Club of Rome and Global 2 000 Reports, have added detail and new dimensions to his argument, but the basic message remains the same.

The statistics are daunting. The human population took 4 million years to reach 1 000 million in 1850, doubling to 2 000 million in 1925,

THE THREE WORLDS

	First World	Second World	Third World
1985			
✳ **Population, millions**	774	399	3 669
✳ **Population as % of world total**	16	8	76
2000			
✳ **Population, millions**	828	446	4 853
✳ **Population as % of world total**	13	8	79
1980-1985			
✳ **Annual growth rate, %**	0,6	0,9	2,2
1985			
✳ **Percentage of population under 15 years age**	21	25	40
✳ **Percentage of global economic product**	69	12	19

Chart 6

reaching 3 000 million in 1962, 4 000 million in 1975 and an awesome 5 000 million in 1987. Despite lowered birth rates in many countries, the global population will increase by 1 000 million every 12 years to the middle of the 21st century.

It is not only the absolute numbers that are cause for alarm, but also the rapidity of growth during the past century and the massive disparity in age and wealth between the so-called Developed and Less-Developed Countries.

The situation can be summarized thus: 76% of the world's population live in the Less-Developed Countries (LDCs) or Third World. More than 40% of this population is aged 15 years or younger. The LDCs' total population is increasing by 2,2% per annum, and doubles every 32 years. They generate only 19% of the world's Gross Domestic Product (GDP).

The people of the Developed Countries (DCs), or First World, represent 16% of the world's population and account for 69% of the world's GDP. Their GDP per capita is 13 times higher than that of the LDCs. The DCs have a stable or decreasing population. It is ageing as the baby boomers of the late 1940s and 1950s become middle-aged. The median age of the DCs' populations will be 38 in the year 2025, almost a generation older than that of the LDCs, which will be 22.

The world can thus be divided into the Rich Old Millions (DC, First World) and the Poor Young Billions (LDC, Third World). The 'Second World' of the centrally planned economies of the USSR and Eastern Europe, with only 8% of the population and 12% of the global GDP, lies between these two extremes.

On a continental scale, Africa has the world's highest population growth rate (2,8% per annum), which doubles the population every 25 years. In contrast to the rest of the world, where food production has outpaced population growth over the past two decades, per capita agricultural production in Africa has decreased by 13% over the same period. As a result, more than 50% of sub-Saharan Africa's people live in conditions of abject poverty. Even if they survive a malnourished childhood, hundreds of millions will never have the opportunity to realize their full human potential.

Even under the best future scenarios for Africa, the situation will worsen for several more decades. Furthermore, the prevalence of civil war, corruption and the lack of infrastructure for distribution will continue to obstruct supplies of food from the DCs' surplus stocks to the worst affected areas.

Malnutrition and related afflictions at present account for over five million deaths annually in Africa. This is equivalent to 45 jumbo jet crashes every day, with no survivors, and with more than 50% of the victims under 15 years of age.

Forty-five 'Helderbergs' or 'Lockerbies' a day, every day – and not a tear shed!

While some African countries are forging new agricultural and economic policies which promise to boost food production, widespread starvation will be prevalent in Africa for many decades to come. The demands for resources by these impoverished people – 870 million by the year 2 000 – will accelerate deforestation, soil erosion and desertification and intensify the impact of floods, droughts, cyclones and other natural disasters.

With no significant change in direction, an Africa burdened with a massive, youthful and poorly educated population will not be able to participate in the industrial and technological renaissance of the 21st century. The new technologies on which the future of humanity will depend will not be transferable to a continent submerged in an apparently inescapable mire of physical and intellectual impoverishment. A rich, rapidly developing South Africa could have to carry an ever increasing burden of refugees.

Before moving off the population topic, we must comment on two currently fashionable notions. The first is that neither human numbers nor population growth rates pose a threat to the future wellbeing of mankind. This view, promoted by iconoclastic American economists, such as the University of Illinois' Julian Simon, asserts that, other things being equal, more people mean more ideas, more food, more energy, more health services, more national parks. Regrettably, other things are not equal! Although this hypothesis holds within the dynamic economies of the First World, it does not hold in the Third World.

The second notion assumes that because the demographic projections of the 1930s and 1940s were so inaccurate, we need not worry about current projections of a global population of 10 billion in the mid-21st century. It is argued that the global population will reach a lower plateau much sooner, as the innovative masses of the Third World transform current poverty into future affluence.

Such assertions are both ill-founded and irresponsible. They ignore the momentum built into young, rapidly growing populations. The flywheel of population growth does not come to a sudden stop on reaching a breakeven fertility rate of 210 babies per 100 child-bearing women.

India provides a classic example. Even if a miracle of family planning during the next 30 years were to reduce Indian families from the present 4,6 to the 2,1 children per family needed to reach zero population growth, it would take almost a century to stabilize the Indian population. By that time the population would have increased from today's 800 million to over 2 billion – more than the entire global population of 1925.

We will return to aspects of human population growth in greater detail later. It is necessary to emphasize, however, that almost every facet of environmental quality, and of sociopolitical and economic development, is a function of human numbers. Human numbers could kill the world. How paradoxical that the advance of modern medicine, which saves the lives of infants and extends the lives of the elderly, may one day prove to have assisted in man's downfall!

THE INVISIBLE THREAT OF GLOBAL WARMING

In 1890 a Swede, Svante Arrhenius, described the interaction between the concentration of atmospheric carbon dioxide (CO_2) and air temperature. He drew attention to the possible long-term impact that the coal-dependent Industrial Revolution would have on global climates. A century later, his predictions look as if they might be true.

The insidious, invisible and largely unrecognized consequences of human population growth are clearly reflected in increases in atmospheric carbon dioxide and methane levels since 1600 AD. These trends were revealed from an analysis of air bubbles trapped in Antarctic ice. The remarkable similarity with the trends in human population growth are more than coincidental.

The changes in atmospheric carbon dioxide and global mean surface temperature over the past 160 000 years have also been plotted from an analysis of Antarctic ice cores. While the close congruence of patterns does not prove conclusively that past changes in the climate were induced by carbon dioxide, it does demonstrate that variations in carbon dioxide have formed an integral link with climate.

Carbon dioxide is one of the most important gases in the atmosphere, even though it accounts for a mere 0,03%. Carbon dioxide plays a key role in determining the Earth's climate. It lets through virtually all the incoming short-wave solar energy, but traps and retains much of the long-wave energy that the Earth radiates out towards space: hence the popular analogy of a 'greenhouse effect'.

The atmospheric concentration of carbon dioxide has increased rapidly since the beginning of the Industrial Revolution, and most

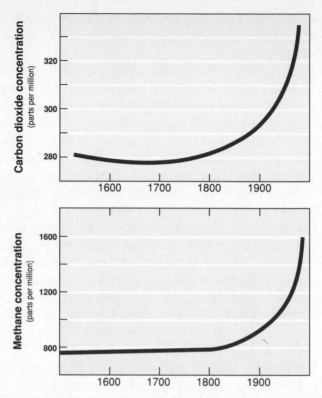

Chart 7 · Atmospheric carbon dioxide and methane levels since 1600 (Source: Pearman 1988)

dramatically this century with the gigantic increase in the use of fossil fuels and the deforestation of the tropics. Fossil fuel combustion currently emits 5,4 billion tonnes of carbon into the atmosphere every year. In addition, the cutting down of the world's forests increases the level of atmospheric carbon by between one and two billion tonnes annually, both by reducing the photosynthetic uptake of carbon dioxide and through the release of carbon from the burning of felled timber. A third major contributor to atmospheric carbon dioxide is the accelerated decomposition of the organic matter in the soil of deforested and newly cultivated land.

Whereas the level of atmospheric carbon dioxide in 1850 amounted to 280 parts per million, it has now increased to 348 parts. Unchecked,

26

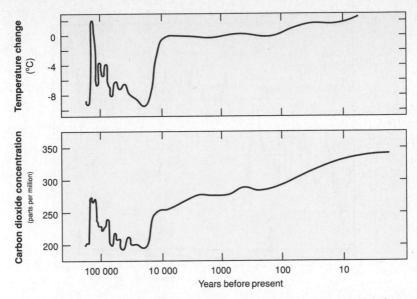

Chart 8 · Relative change in atmospheric carbon dioxide concentration and global temperature during the past 160 000 years (Source: Pearman 1988)

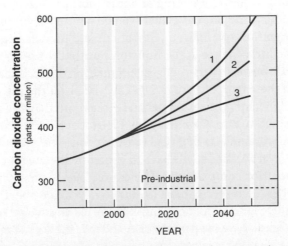

Chart 9 · Predicted growth of atmospheric carbon dioxide concentration under different energy-use scenarios: (1) 2,3% annual growth to 2050, (2) current growth rate, (3) 1,5% to 2000, thereafter no further growth (Source: Pearman 1988)

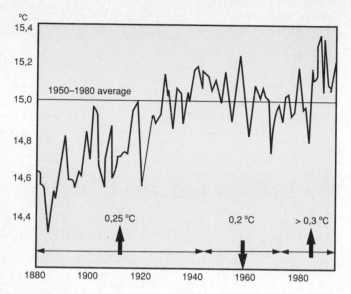

Chart 10 · Mean global temperature over the past 100 years (Source: *New Scientist* 1988)

it could well reach 600 parts per million by the year 2050. The surmised result is a steady warming of our planet, projected to rise to a mean 3 °C above the present global average within the lifetime of the present generation of children. Global climate models suggest that there will be little change at the Equator, but that the poles may well become 7 °C warmer, with a consequent melting of the polar icecaps. The rates of these temperature changes may be faster than at any other time in human history, even greater and more rapid than the major oscillations which took place during the Pleistocene Ice Ages.

While the worst effects of global warming could be a problem with which future generations will have to contend, the current position gives no room for complacency. The annual average temperature of the globe has increased almost continuously since the Industrial Revolution. Despite a slight cooling in the 1950s and 1960s, later temperature patterns have been on the rise. Indeed, the six warmest years recorded since reliable global temperature observations began 100 years ago occurred in the 1980s. The decade itself is the hottest on record, with 1988 being the hottest year of the century.

While the warming of the atmosphere might be the first and most tangible consequence of the greenhouse effect, many secondary impacts are conjectured. These could reach significant levels by 2050 and include:

- Major changes in global and regional climates.
- Crop losses necessitating changes in agricultural patterns.
- Increased frequency and amplitude of extreme weather events.
- Rising sea levels.
- Spread of diseases and pests.
- Rapid losses of species.
- Desertification.

Little wonder that global warming has been described by World Watch Institute's Lester Brown as a "tragedy of the commons writ large".

The most profound influence could be on global and regional climates. While some regions might be wetter and others drier than at present, all regions are expected to become warmer. Projections for South Africa indicate a generally warmer, drier situation, where soil moisture conditions in the Highveld grain basket might be 11-18% drier than at present.

Even more significant may be a shift in seasonality. The south-west Cape, presently receiving its rains in winter, could become a summer rainfall region, with unfavourable consequences for its wine and wheat industries.

Shifts in atmospheric pressure gradients and wind circulation patterns, coupled with changes in ocean currents, could markedly alter the distribution, abundance and availability of marine resources. Africa's largest fishing industry, in the region of the Benguela Current, could face collapse on account of a reduction in the supply of cold, nutrient-rich upwelled water. At the same time, incursions of warm surface water along the west coast of southern Africa, a phenomenon known as the 'Benguela El Niño', could occur with greater frequency – if not continuously.

While a warmer world richer in carbon dioxide should generally be able to grow more food, some nations would be winners and others losers. This would introduce the potential for profound changes in economic rankings.

Much of the North American grain belt could suffer permanent drought. A 1 °C increase in temperature plus a 10% decrease in rainfall could reduce the wheat crop by one-fifth – with adverse consequences not only for North Americans, but for the more than 100 countries that now benefit from the USA's grain surplus.

The USSR, by contrast, could merely push its main grain-growing area northwards into a warmed-up Siberia, which possesses suitable soils. In Australia, the optimum bioclimate for wheat might shift onto unsuitable soils, or into the Tasman Sea, changing the country from an exporter to an importer of wheat. In contrast, the area suited to maize production might increase.

The loss of crops through a changed bioclimate is but one component of a plethora of potential crises in the future of food production. The increased incidence and rate of the spread of diseases, pests and plagues and the loss of genetic diversity are of even greater concern.

More than 90% of the world's food is derived from fewer than 20 species of plants. The genetic make-up of these, which enables them to adapt to changing conditions of temperature, moisture, nutrients and disease organisms, is limited. There is a widely held but erroneous view that plants and animals, once domesticated, are no longer dependent on their wild relatives. However, plant breeders especially have to make frequent use of the disease- and drought-resistant qualities of wild species. Rapid changes in their habitats could result in a loss of the genetic diversity locked up in these wild relatives of crop plants. The potential of breeding new strains and varieties capable of adapting to a changed globe would be severely restricted.

The destruction of tropical rainforests is already driving 100 species of animals and plants into extinction every day. According to tropical botanist Peter Raven, nearly half a million species will be lost in this spasm of extinction by the end of the century, at rates 1 000 times more than the pace that has prevailed since the beginning of time. Global warming would greatly increase even this pace, creating a game of 'ecological chairs' in which species swop habitats as ecological conditions change, with some dropping out as suitable habitats disappear.

The south-west Cape's remnant patches of lowland fynbos, the richest plant communities in the world, would be the hardest hit of all. Most of these occur as small islands in a sea of agricultural and urban development. The chances of individual species dispersing back and forth as habitat conditions change is thus greatly reduced. Even the narrow corridors provided by roadside verges, stream banks and hedgerows have been diminished by ploughing, burning or other disturbances. Many if not most species of proteas and ericas and their associated biota will be at risk of extinction if global warming occurs.

But this is not the end of the bad news.

The rise in frequency and scale of extreme events like droughts, floods, hailstorms and hurricanes – which would occur as the global climate moved through a series of temporary states to a new equilibrium – would have a severe impact on infrastructure, agriculture and reinsurance. All Third World and most First World nations would simply not be able to prevent or cover the costs of the natural disasters which might follow in the wake of the changing global climate.

The melting of the polar icecaps and the expansion of the water of warmer oceans could cause sea levels to rise by 0,5-1,5 metres by the middle of the 21st century. The impact of the existing processes of

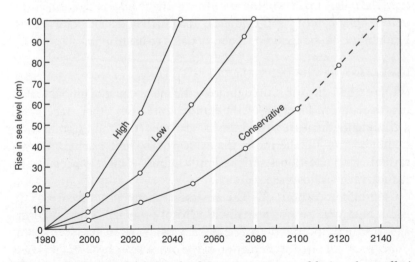

Chart 11 · Predictions of global sea-level rise as a consequence of the 'greenhouse effect'

coastal subsidence would be accelerated. Without extremely expensive precautions, much of the Netherlands would be flooded, together with half of Florida and huge sections of other low-lying areas. Venice and Bangkok would finally drown.

The combined effects of sea-level rise and coastal subsidence imply a scenario in which more than 30% of the arable land of Egypt and Bangladesh could be inundated. A single cyclone drowned 300 000 people in Bangladesh in 1970. Millions could perish in the wake of cyclones following even minor increases in sea level.

South Africa, with its current passion for the development of marinas, would not remain unscathed. Much of the real estate and infrastructural development along our coastline could be at risk by the year 2050. Our position, at the tip of Africa, exposed to the full brunt of the storms generated over the Southern Ocean, makes the South African coastline one of the most vulnerable to the physical impact of a rising sea level.

After listing all these potential woes, we would like to emphasize that they still lie in the realm of hypothesis. The rising concentration of carbon dioxide in the atmosphere is fact; that it is the prime cause of global warming over the last two hundred years is not yet scientifically proven. But, if the future of the globe is not to be placed at risk, the policy makers of the world are going to have to make hard decisions on apparently soft evidence. Too much is at stake for even low probabilities to be ignored. Nobody courts catastrophe.

DEPLETION OF THE OZONE LAYER

While carbon dioxide is thought to be the major cause of global warming, accounting for 49% of the temperature rise, other trace gases including methane (18%) and the halocarbons (14%) add significantly to the process. Furthermore, the halocarbons, such as chlorofluorocarbon, have additional serious implications – most especially the reduction of stratospheric ozone.

Chlorofluorocarbons (CFCs) are inert chemicals, discovered in 1930. They are used principally as aerosol propellants and refrigerants, and in the production of rigid foam insulators such as styrofoam. Concern about possible depletion of the ozone layer by CFCs was first voiced in 1974. Research has since indicated that the chlorine released

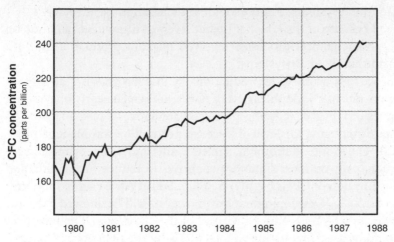

Chart 12 · Atmospheric CFC concentration at Cape Point (Source: Brunke 1988)

from CFCs rises to the stratosphere and reduces the amount of ozone, which shields the planet from harmful ultraviolet radiation.

Because CFCs have an average atmospheric lifetime of 75 years and do not break down in the lower atmosphere, they move slowly to the stratosphere where higher energy radiation strikes them and they release chlorine. Once freed, the chlorine acts as a catalyst, repeatedly combining with and breaking apart ozone molecules.

The long atmospheric lifetime of CFCs implies that their impact on the ozone layer will continue into the mid-21st century, even if the production and use of CFCs were to stop today.

During the past few years, researchers in the Antarctic have identified a growing hole in the ozone layer of the stratosphere over the South Pole, with localized depletion of as much as 50%. This hole tends to shift about over the southern sky, so that increased ultraviolet radiation potentially threatens both marine and terrestrial life in the southern hemisphere. South Africa is especially vulnerable.

Human beings, when exposed to increased ultraviolet radiation, are more likely to contract non-melanoma skin cancer and cataracts. A 1% rise in ultraviolet radiation is reckoned to produce a 2-3% increase in the frequency of skin cancer. Adverse effects could also include an increase in the incidence of malignant melanomas and possible damage to immune systems. Plant and aquatic life might be adversely influenced because of the effect of higher levels of ultraviolet radiation on the photochemical processes involved in plant production in both marine and land ecosystems.

Since 1983, worldwide production of CFCs has grown at an average annual rate of 5%, doubling every 14 years. By 1986 nearly one million tonnes of CFCs were being produced annually. In 1987 a small step towards reducing the level of trace gas production was made in Montreal. The Montreal Protocol, agreed to after nearly five years of negotiation, calls on most signatory countries to reduce production and consumption of CFCs by 50% by 1999. South Africa signed the Protocol in 1989. Developing nations, however, will be allowed a decade longer in which to reduce their use of the chemicals. The net effect should be a 35% reduction in total CFCs by the turn of the century.

Nevertheless, the Montreal Protocol is regarded as hopelessly inadequate. Most First World countries are calling for a total ban on CFCs by the year 2000. Third World countries, currently responsible for less than 25% of CFC emissions, have objected to the proposal. China plans a tenfold increase in CFC production by the end of the century. The Protocol is thus little more than a token gesture. Perhaps the meeting in Helsinki in early May 1989, with representatives from 86 countries favouring the total ban requested by First World countries, augurs well for the future. But the Helsinki accord includes a demand for a United Nations fund, financed by industrialized countries, to help the developing world to adjust their economies to cope without the use of CFCs.

A WAY OUT

What is needed is an extensive and concerted international programme to reduce our dependence on fossil fuels. There are good reasons to believe that such a change can and will take place over the next few decades. Recent advances in the increased energy efficiency of cars and gas turbines, and in the development of superconductors, photovoltaics and biotechnology, promise to reduce the level of dependence on fossil fuels substantially. Safer and smaller sources of nuclear power are particularly relevant. Improved agricultural and forestry practices could reverse the current trends in tropical deforestation.

Even the increasing levels of atmospheric carbon dioxide might be turned to good use by increasing the efficiency of plant growth, helping to mop up much of the excess carbon dioxide available.

So all is not lost, especially if we can advance from the energy-sapping technologies of the 20th century to new, benign technologies in the 21st century. This will only occur, however, if we choose the course suggested by World Resources Institute's Gus Speth: a transformation, unprecedented in scope and pace, to technologies that facilitate economic growth while sharply reducing the pressures on the natural environment.

Most importantly, we must make the free-enterprise market mechanism work for us and use it to guide research and development and technological innovation. The last thing one wants is to have these functions micro-managed by government. The taxpayer has traditionally borne the brunt of the costs of environmental damage. This burden could now become an opportunity for profit for the imaginative investor in new technologies.

4 South Africa in the 1980s: The Decade the Environment Hit Back

To most South Africans, especially the poor, the 1980s will be remembered as 'the decade the environment hit back'. Never before in recorded history has the country endured such a succession of droughts, floods, hailstorms, veld fires and locust outbreaks. Severe rural and urban degradation as well as poverty are the consequences. Not even in the 1930s did South Africa experience natural disasters of the diversity and dimension of those of the last ten years.

The decade began with an extended drought, punctuated only by the tragic flood at Laingsburg. Elsewhere, dams dried up, water was rationed as never before and rivers had to be diverted to supplement supplies to industry. For the first time, many affluent South Africans experienced the bitter taste of water shortages familiar to the vast majority of the nation's populace.

Livestock succumbed in tens of thousands. In KwaZulu alone, more than 40 000 cattle died in 1983. The national maize harvest dropped from 14 million tonnes in 1981 to 4 million tonnes in 1983. Hot, dry conditions increased the risk of veld fires. Hundreds of thousands of hectares of the highly flammable fynbos of the western Cape mountains burnt, often with loss of life and property.

Then, once again, devasting floods hit the country. Cyclone Domoina in February 1984 was followed by a succession of floods in southern Natal and the western Cape. In 1987 Natal was once again hit and in 1988 virtually the whole country was awash. Hundreds of lives were lost and damage worth hundreds of millions of rands to property was sustained. Dams were filled overnight; some burst and took with them bridges, roads and railways.

During the month of March 1988, the Orange River carried more than 80 million tonnes of silt and sediment into the Atlantic – more than had been carried to sea during the preceding five years. At the height of the flood, more water passed through the river mouth in three

NATURAL DISASTERS IN SOUTH AFRICA IN THE 1980s

1981 Laingsburg flood, 114 lives lost
1981 Drought relief, R180 m
1982 Hail damage to crops, R68 m
1983 Drop in maize production from 14 m to 4 m tonnes
1984 Domoina floods, 109 lives lost, R210 m damage
1986 Windstorm damage, E Tvl, R65 m
1986 Hail damage to crops, R98 m
1986 Sandstorms, E Cape
1986 Locust swarms, R40 m control costs
1987 Natal floods, 487 lives lost, R1 100 m damage
1988 Floods, Cape/OFS, R600 m damage
1988 Veld fires, Western Cape, 150 000 ha burnt
1988 Drought relief, R396 m

Chart 13

days than is used by the entire Pretoria-Witwatersrand-Vereeniging complex in a year.

In the wake of the floods, the hardship of life in the squatter camps intensified. Polluted water caused cholera, dysentery and death. Landslides destroyed thousands of already pitiful dwellings. Subsidies relating to drought, floods and agriculture raised the farming debt to over R14 000 million – equal to the gross value of South Africa's agricultural production in 1988.

Even the most sophisticated technologies of the 20th century could not buffer us from the environment's response to Earth's mismanagement. Our dependence on a harmonious relationship with our habitat became obvious to all.

Much of the environmental damage of the 1980s would have been averted by a healthy, resilient complex of soils, vegetation and animal life. We have had to pay the price for over a century of careless environmental management and South Africa's unique experiment in social engineering. A few examples of the reduction in environmental quality illustrate the point.

37

Soil erosion remains a serious problem over much of South Africa, notwithstanding almost four decades of concerted effort by dedicated conservationists and enormous state expenditure. Annual soil losses are estimated at 300-400 million tonnes, nearly three tonnes per hectare. If this soil were loaded onto seven-tonne trucks placed bumper to bumper, they would extend seven and a half times around the circumference of the globe. If the plant nutrients such as nitrogen, potassium and phosphorus, carried to the sea by our rivers every year, were to be entirely replaced by commercial fertilizers, the cost would exceed R1 000 million.

Each year, for every tonne of maize, wheat, sugar or other agricultural crop produced, South Africa as a whole loses 20 tonnes of soil. Whereas crops are renewable, soil to all intents and purposes is not. The mean rate of soil formation in Africa is less than 0,1 tonne per hectare per year, so that the current rate of loss is more than 30 times the rate of soil formation. Almost three million hectares have been rendered unusable as a result of severe donga and sheet erosion. In financial terms, this is equivalent to a permanent loss of assets valued at over R1 500 million – a figure which does not include the loss of natural fertilizers quoted above.

Records of soil loss from major catchments show that most of the topsoil and accumulated sediments were washed down to the sea during the early part of the 20th century. The estimated annual soil loss from the Orange River catchment dropped from 120 million tonnes in 1920 to 35 million tonnes in 1935. Since the 1960s, following the construction of the vast H. F. Verwoerd and P. K. le Roux dams, as well as many thousands of farm dams, soil loss to the sea has dropped to below 20 million tonnes per annum – with the exception of extreme events such as the floods of 1988. However, the actual rate of soil loss from individual farms has not dropped significantly. The network of dams is merely holding back millions of tonnes of sediment and silt.

Erosion in Natal increased steadily from colonial times until the mid-20th century, but has tended to decrease over the past four decades. Nonetheless, the rate of erosional loss from the Tugela catchment is still 20 times higher than that occurring over the past million years.

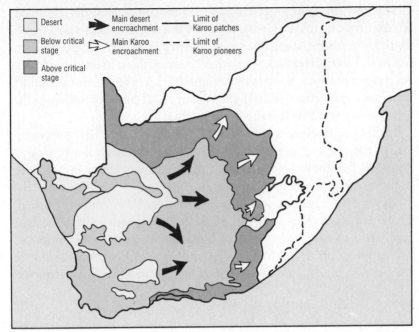

Chart 14 · Desertification and Karoo encroachment over South Africa (Source: Acocks 1975)

VELD DETERIORATION – THE EXPANSION OF THE KAROO

The frequency of droughts and the deterioration of the condition of the veld in the Karoo has been the subject of comment and commissions of inquiry since the mid-19th century. Despite much research and debate, the processes involved and the rates of change are still poorly understood. There is little doubt, however, that the long-term productivity of the region has been substantially reduced, and that the general patterns, as described by pioneer ecologist John Acocks 30 years ago, are real.

Marked fluctuations in the condition of the veld in the Karoo, which are linked to wet and dry rainfall phases, mask the steady deterioration of this resource. On it our wool and mutton industry is based. A 'safe' stocking rate for the Karoo is estimated to lie between 7,0 and 7,5 million sheep. The present sheep population is about 10 million.

39

The bushveld and grassveld systems are similarly under pressure. An excessive increase in woody species as a result of veld mismanagement has rendered three million hectares of bushveld useless for grazing by domestic livestock – another R1 500 million in lost assets. The carrying capacity of a further 14 million hectares of savanna is rapidly decreasing on account of bush encroachment. This is equivalent to the total area of the TBVC states!

Studies in the eastern Cape Thornveld have shown that the condition of the veld is at present only 49% of its real potential for carrying domestic livestock. Despite this, the current stocking rate has been found to be 1,5 times too high.

The extensive grasslands of the Highveld are also in poor condition. Grassland researchers have estimated that at present only 10% of our grasslands consists of the mix of high-quality grasses best suited to beef production. In addition, as much as 60% of our grassland is in poor condition, unable to meet sustained production requirements.

THE ONWARD MARCH OF INVASIVE PLANTS

Invasive plants, both alien and indigenous, are a further major problem in South Africa. Jointed cactus currently infests over 800 000 hectares. Nassella tussock, an unpalatable, aggressively competitive grass from South America, covers 87 000 hectares. Various woody invasives such as acacias, hakeas and pines have spread over one million hectares of natural veld.

Jointed cactus, a spiny cactus which injures the feet and mouths of sheep and goats, is a serious problem to the wool and mohair farmers of the eastern Cape, severely reducing the profits of these industries. More than R10 million is spent annually on combating the weed.

The woody acacias, pines and hakeas of the south-west and southern Cape constitute both an aesthetic and an economic problem. They are spreading rapidly through both lowland and mountain fynbos, shading out many sensitive erica, protea, gladiolus and similar species. They are thus threatening South Africa's wildflower industry, with an estimated total revenue of R20 million per annum. Together, alien plants diminish the capital value of this country's agricultural sector by several billions of rands.

The South African government is reported to have spent more than R40 million trying to bring the 1986-87 locust swarms under control. Some 630 000 hectares of land were sprayed and over 6 600 tonnes of insecticide were used in the two 'outbreak' seasons. Eighty-five per cent of this was the persistent benzene hexachloride (BHC) – a substance normally banned from use in South Africa.

Spraying operations conducted over the past 80 years have not solved or even reduced the problem of locusts. Indeed, the bid to exterminate the brown locust has had some unforeseen consequences. The species' population dynamics have changed, with shorter but more frequent outbreaks occurring.

Before 1907, control was mechanical and outbreaks typically lasted about 13 years, with periods between outbreaks of about 11 years. Chemical spraying was first tried in 1907, and by 1920 large changes in locust behaviour were apparent. Outbreak periods fell to between six and seven years, with seven to eight years between outbreaks. However, the 'success' of these measures was partially impaired by the fencing of farms and by the control of locust predators such as jackals by means of strychnine. In the 1960s, spraying became more sophisticated. The pattern now appears to be two years of outbreak separated by two-year intervals.

Many scientists and farmers argue that the financial and environmental costs of the control operations far outweigh the potential damage of locust swarms.

THE WORLD'S RICHEST FLORA AT RISK

South Africa's floral wealth is one of its richest natural assets and tourist attractions, yet many species are under threat of extinction. A detailed survey of the approximately 20 300 species of southern African flowering plants indicates that the survival of 2 373 species is currently at risk.

The flora of the Cape Floristic Kingdom, centred in the south-west Cape, is the most severely threatened. The Cape Floristic Kingdom is one of the six major subdivisions of the world's flora. It is by far the smallest in area, but in terms of the diversity of its plant families and species it is incredibly rich. The Cape Peninsula, only 47 000 hectares in extent, possesses 2 256 indigenous species – more than half the flora of eastern North America.

Out of a total of approximately 6 000 fynbos species confined to an area of about nine million hectares in the Cape, 1 621 species are included in the threatened category. Of these, 137 species face imminent extinction. The majority of the threatened species survive in remnant patches of fynbos in an area of less than 1,8 million hectares, only 1,5% of South Africa's land area.

But far more worrying is that many of the threatened species are confined to habitats facing drastic alteration. One such group of 28 endangered species survives in a remnant patch of coastal fynbos amounting to 4 500 hectares, reduced in the past century from an original habitat of more than 600 000 hectares.

A changing global environment could move the majority of the Cape's 1 621 threatened plant species from the category of 'endangered' to that of 'extinct'. And as the World Wide Fund for Nature (WWF) adage goes, 'extinction is forever'.

5 Environmental 'Rules of the Game' for South Africa

The scenario planner's dictum states that 'the future is not what it used to be'. The world is in constant flux. The future is unknown, indeed unknowable. But there are ground rules which are highly unlikely to change in the medium term – to the year 2000 – and which fix the limits within which future environmental scenarios can be developed. We call these the environmental 'rules of the game'. They include:

– The natural diversity and richness of South Africa's landscapes, habitats, fauna and flora.
– The climate and weather patterns which characterize the country on a regional scale.
– The distribution of key natural resources – minerals, water and arable land.
– The dynamics and settlement patterns of our human population.
– Agricultural and forestry resources.
– The marine environment.
– Economic growth and consumption patterns.

DIVERSITY: A WORLD IN ONE COUNTRY

Our popular tourism slogan is that South Africa is 'a world in one country'. To the ecologist at least, this is true. Our geographic position, between the warm Agulhas Current on the east and the cold Benguela Current on the west, accounts for a diverse range of climatic conditions. A narrow coastal plain, steep escarpment and extensive plateau produce great topographic gradients. A mix of tropical to temperate climates and habitats that range from rainforest to desert means that South Africa is blessed with the richest diversity of plant life of any region on earth. The animal life of South Africa is similarly rich in variety.

Our flora includes more than 20 300 species of flowering plants and

ENVIRONMENTAL 'RULES OF THE GAME' FOR SOUTH AFRICA

* Natural diversity and richness
* Variability in climate and weather patterns
* Population dynamics: First World/Third World dichotomy
* Mass urbanization
* Agriculture divided: prosperity and poverty
* Mismatch of industrial growth points and water availability
* Coal, energy and atmospheric pollution
* Restricted access to domestic energy and water
* Limits to growth in the marine environment
* Economic growth and consumption patterns

Chart 15

many hundreds of ferns, mosses, lichens and fungi, while our animal kingdom includes some 800 species of birds, 243 species of mammals, 84 species of amphibians, 286 species of reptiles, 632 species of butterflies and tens of thousands of species of other insects. More than 580 national parks and nature reserves, totalling over 7,2 million hectares, have been set aside to protect our diverse flora and fauna. Nearly 97%

DIVERSITY: A WORLD IN ONE COUNTRY

* Diversity of climate, topography, ecosystems
* Over 20 300 species of flowering plants, 800 of birds, 243 of mammals, 84 of amphibians, 286 of reptiles
* 580 protected areas, 7,2 million ha
* Tourism industry worth R3 150 m, 35% forex

Chart 16

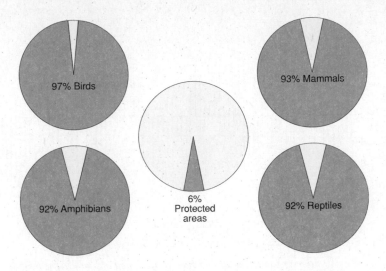

Chart 17 · Percentage of different vertebrate groups recorded from the 6% of South Africa's land area falling within national parks and nature reserves

of the birds, 93% of mammals, 92% of amphibians and 92% of our reptiles are included in this protected area network, which makes it one of the most effective systems of its kind in the world.

The rich diversity of landscapes and wildlife that South Africa boasts is the prime drawcard of our tourism industry. In 1987 this was valued at R3 150 million, of which 35% was in the form of foreign exchange from nearly one million overseas visitors. Tourism contributed 2,4% of our total foreign exchange earnings in 1987. It is expected that the number of foreign visitors will increase by as much as 15% annually for several years.

VARIABILITY IN CLIMATE AND WEATHER

South Africa enjoys one of the most pleasant and healthiest climates in the world – attractive to humans, that is, but not necessarily to crops!

The average annual rainfall of about 497 mm for South Africa as a whole is well below the world average of 860 mm. A comparatively narrow region along the eastern and southern coastlines is moderately well watered, but the greater part of the interior and the west of the country is arid or semi-arid.

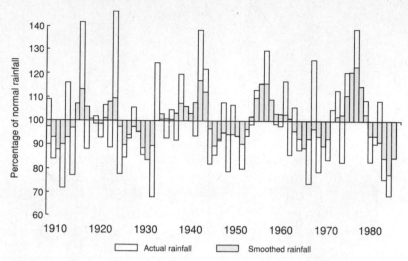

Chart 18 · Variation in rainfall in the summer rainfall area of South Africa (Source: Tyson 1987)

Sixty-five per cent of the country has an annual rainfall of less than 500 mm, which is usually regarded as the minimum rainfall needed for crop farming without irrigation. Twenty-one per cent of the country receives less than 200 mm. Over most of the country the annual potential evaporation, which ranges from about 1 100 mm to more than 3 000 mm, is well in excess of the annual rainfall. South Africa is, by any standard, an arid country.

Despite popular opinion, no long-term decrease or increase in rainfall has been shown from the analysis of our long-term rainfall records.

CONSEQUENCES OF SOUTH AFRICA'S RAINFALL PERIODICITY

❋ **Expansion of cultivated lands into marginal areas**
❋ **Pulsed expansion of Karoo and desertification**
❋ **Provision of subsidies exacerbates veld deterioration**
❋ **Veld recovery insufficient to reverse deterioration**
❋ **The 1990s could be relatively wet**

Chart 19

But a feature of South Africa's rainfall is the apparent existence of cycles of wet and dry spells. Eighteen-year cycles of approximately nine dry and nine wet years occur in the summer rainfall area. Alternating spells have commenced in 1944 (dry); 1953 (wet); 1962 (dry); 1971 (wet); 1980 (dry) and 1988 (wet). The duration, intensity and distribution of such spells vary widely.

The winter rainfall region of the south-west Cape often displays the opposite trend to the wet and dry cycles of the summer rainfall area. Thus the interior and eastern half of South Africa might be experiencing an extended drought while the south-west Cape enjoys above-average rains.

It is unwise to develop broad generalizations from these trends, which provide the kind of wisdom that comes only with hindsight. But, from a close look at the cycles in the summer rainfall region, we have learnt that the rainfall patterns do have important environmental consequences. Among them are that:

- Soil erosion rates during wet cycles are up to three times higher than rates during dry cycles.
- Marginal areas are cultivated during wet spells, which leads to the collapse of crop farming systems during subsequent dry spells.
- The Karoo expands eastward in pulses following successive dry cycles.
- Subsidies are provided to tide livestock farmers over dry spells, with the result that they do not reduce stock numbers when they should.
- Consequently veld recovery through a wet spell is insufficient to reverse the long-term trend of deterioration.

If present patterns are maintained, much of the 1990s will be relatively wet. We may have nine years of grace in which to launch new initiatives before the lean years of the next dry cycle usher in the new century!

POPULATION DYNAMICS: FIRST WORLD/THIRD WORLD DICHOTOMY

The South African population is expected to increase from 32,1 million in 1985 to 45,1 million in the year 2000, with the black component

SOUTH AFRICA'S POPULATION (1 000s), 1985 AND 2000

1985	Urban	Rural	Total
White	4 272	528	4 800
Asian	815	81	896
Coloured	2 260	676	2 936
Black	8 930	14 570	23 500
Total	16 277	15 855	32 132

2000	Urban	Rural	Total
White	5 147	271	5 418
Asian	1 079	45	1 124
Coloured	3 298	366	3 664
Black	26 175	8 725	34 900
Total	35 699	9 407	45 106

Chart 20

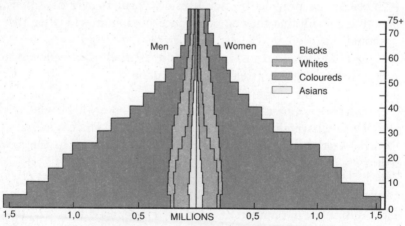

Chart 21 · Age structure of the South African population, 1980

48

SOUTH AFRICAN POPULATION DYNAMICS

* Black increase by 2000 greater than white, coloured and Asian by 2100

* Socioeconomic progress essential for black demographic transition

* Economically active population of 2000 already born

* Global division into Rich Old Millions/Poor Young Billions applicable to SA

Chart 22

increasing from 73% to 77%. The age structure of the black population will change slightly: those below 15 years old dropping from 43% to 39% of the total – still a young profile. The equivalent ratio for whites will fall from 27% to 20%. These figures are unlikely to change much because the mothers of all the children to be born before the year 2000 have already been born themselves.

The separation of South Africa into First World and Third World components is nowhere more strongly reflected than in the patterns of population growth. The major portion of the black population still adheres to the tradition of large families, tied as it is to the economic standards of the Third World. High fertility rates and relatively low mortality rates because of access to First World medicines and infrastructure produce a black population growth rate of 2,72% per annum. If this rate is maintained, the black population will double within 25 years.

The First World sector of the population has benefited from superior employment, education, nutrition and housing conditions. Represented by the white, Asian and higher income coloured populations, this sector has a growth rate of only 0,65% per annum and a doubling time of more than 100 years.

In view of the existing differences in population size, the increase in numbers of the black population over the next decade will almost certainly be greater than that of all the other population groups combined in the next 100 years.

49

Changes in total fertility rate (TFR) within different socioeconomic groups and nations defy the most sophisticated demographic models. Often, unexpected and rapid changes in TFR patterns occur within the space of a few decades. In South Africa, the coloured people's TFR dropped from 6,8 to 3,5 births per woman in the period between 1960 and 1980, leading to a fall in their population growth rate from 3,3% to 1,9% per annum. Contributing to this decrease in TFR was the rapid economic progress experienced by the coloured population in the 1960s and 1970s.

Currently, whites earn nearly ten times the per capita income of blacks. Even in a scenario where the per capita income of blacks will double by the year 2000, the disparity will remain very large. For the foreseeable future, therefore, the First World/Third World dichotomy of 'Rich Old Millions' and 'Poor Young Billions' will continue to apply in South Africa. But, these facts should not deter us from closing the gap. A substantial improvement in socioeconomic conditions is needed within the next decade to ensure that the black population makes the transition to a modest population growth rate by the year 2000. Otherwise, South Africa will be interminably locked into a descending spiral of overpopulation and poverty.

MASS URBANIZATION

The 20th century has seen an unprecedented flood of people moving from rural to urban areas. The number of cities in the world with populations of more than 100 000 people increased from 50 in 1800 to 900 in 1950. More than a quarter of the global population will live in cities exceeding one million people by the end of the century.

The rate of urbanization in Africa is the highest in the world. Increasing at a rate of 5,1% per annum, the urban populations will double every 14 years. This raises the spectre of sprawling megacities with shifting young populations and a high incidence of crime. But, on the positive side, if the natural entrepreneurial drive of ordinary people can be encouraged and channelled into constructive activities, the future metropolitan markets of South Africa could be amongst the most exciting in the world. This entrepreneurial drive will not be released until much of the crushing bureaucratic machinery is removed from the marketplace.

URBANIZATION TRENDS

* Urban population in Africa doubles every 14 years
* SA's urban population will increase from 16,2 m in 1985 to 35,7 m in 2000
* 750 000 blacks move to urban areas every year
* Over 1 000 dwelling units need to be constructed every working day to 2000
* Five million blacks without a permanent, legal home

Chart 23

While rural population densities in South Africa are likely to decrease over the next decade, the pace of urbanization will bring extensive changes to the pattern of human settlement. South Africa's urban population is expected to grow from 16,2 million in 1985 to 35,7 million in the year 2000. The proportion of blacks in these figures will increase from 55% to 73% – an addition of 750 000 blacks to the urban population every year to the end of the century. By then 79% of South Africa's population will be urbanized. The Pretoria-Witwatersrand-Vereeniging metropolitan area could be one of the 20 largest megacities in the world by the year 2010.

The urbanization process will continue to place huge demands on resources such as land, water, housing, urban infrastructure and skilled manpower. While the white population had a surplus of 83 000 dwelling units in 1985, the shortfall for blacks was between 550 000 and 850 000.

Some two to three million new dwelling units are needed by the turn of the century, equivalent to the construction of more than 1 000 units per working day to the end of the century. The annual cost of erecting these houses will exceed R7 000 million. Current methods of funding, even if sustained, will supply barely 25% of the need. The situation is further aggravated by the fact that while only 8% of whites need assistance to buy a R20 000 home, no less than 75% of blacks are unable to afford such a home without some form of subsidy.

Five million blacks – one in every five – are thought to be without a permanent, legal home. Some three million of these live in the squatter settlements surrounding major cities. The growth of these squatter settlements is unparalleled in South Africa's history – those that surround Durban are said to rival Mexico City in terms of their rate of expansion through the 1980s.

AGRICULTURE DIVIDED: PROSPERITY AND POVERTY

The scarcity of arable land

The total area of South Africa is 122 million hectares, of which just under 101 million hectares are farmland. Of this only 16,6 million hectares are considered arable, which means land that is suitable for dryland crop production without irrigation. Thus far 13,5 million hectares of arable land have been cultivated for crops, leaving a relatively small amount of low-potential land for future expansion.

The remaining 84 million hectares of nonarable farmland are natural vegetation, used primarily for grazing.

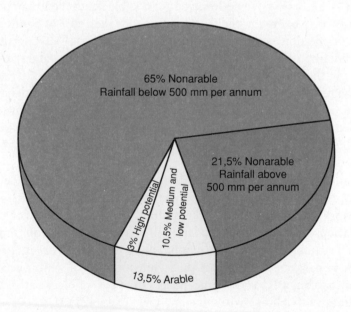

Chart 24 · Land-use potential of South Africa

The poverty of the homelands

The most significant statistic concerning farmland is its distribution between 'white' South Africa and the homelands. The former has 85,4 million hectares and the latter 15,1 million hectares. Of the 85,4 million 'white' hectares, 14,3 million hectares are arable, whilst of the 15,1 million 'homeland' hectares, 2,3 million hectares are arable.

The significance of this distribution becomes apparent when one adds to the equation the fact that 14 million people out of South Africa's population of 33 million are crowded into the homelands. Put another way, 42% of the population is confined to 13% of the land. Compounding the problem is the lack of major industrial centres in the homelands to absorb large numbers of people and relieve the congestion of the countryside. Moreover, some of the communities resettled from 'white' areas have been located on land that is completely unsuitable for farming.

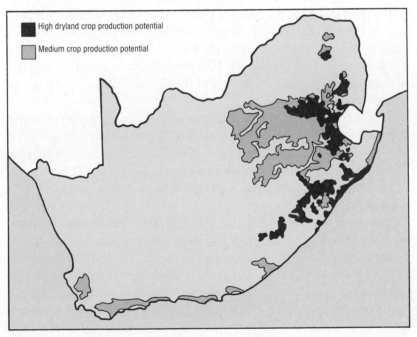

High dryland crop production potential

Medium crop production potential

Chart 25 · Distribution of crop production potential (Source: Scotney 1988)

AGRICULTURE IN THE HOMELANDS

* 6% of SA's agricultural output from 13% of the land
* Less than 10% reaches the market
* Myths of adequate land and farming incompetence
* Population pressures
* Inadequate and unbalanced infrastructure
* Land and cattle as social security, not productive assets

but

* Potential sufficient to meet food needs to the year 2000, if unlocked by free market

Chart 26

Given the shortage of arable land, pressure on it in the homelands is acute. This is reflected in the amount of available arable land per person. In the homelands, it is currently 0,16 hectares per person and will drop to less than 0,1 hectares by the year 2000. This compares to 0,51 hectares per person for the whole of South Africa, which is expected to drop to 0,36 hectares at the end of the century. The global norm is 0,4 hectares per person.

For the small proportion of the black population in the fortunate position of having access to arable land in the homelands, little more than two hectares are available per family. The extremely high population densities and the totally skewed distribution of land have driven black farmers onto marginal land that is often highly erodable. Responsibility for the widespread dongas which scar many homelands cannot, therefore, be attributed solely to local farming methods. They are also the product of ignorant social engineering and the high rate of population growth which accompanies increasing destitution.

The agricultural production of the homelands can meet just 16% of its residents' own food needs. Less than a tenth of the production actually reaches the market, the balance being consumed by the growers themselves. Thus the major portion of the food needs of homeland communities is supplied from sources outside the homelands.

Financial aid and advisory services to agriculture in the homelands have been erratic, often disruptive and wholly inadequate. This broad statement does not imply that valiant efforts have not been made to improve the situation. A group of committed extension officers inside and outside government service have made magnificent contributions, but their lights have been hidden under the bushels of misdirected policies. The ratio of aid to white versus black agriculture was 197:1 between 1910 and 1936. In the 1950s, it improved to 14:1 and in the 1980s to 2:1. These ratios relate to total aid, however, not to aid per farmer. So white farmers are still provided with superior financial and extension aid per head. We are not for one moment suggesting that black farmers (or white ones for that matter) should in future be smothered with welfare. The aid must be channelled into infrastructure and training. Thereafter, the farmers are on their own.

In Transkei, four hectares of arable dryland are required per household for subsistence-level farming in the medium- to high-potential areas. Less than 8% of the farmers have this much land and only 5%

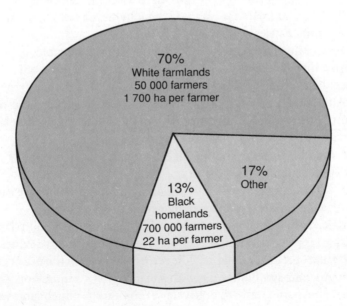

Chart 27 · Distribution of farmland

of Transkei farmers produce maize yields of two tonnes per hectare. This is low by world standards, but it is in fact not dissimilar to the average of white commercial farms.

Despite high unemployment levels in the homelands, labour scarcities can occur during peak periods of crop planting or reaping. Accordingly, 20-30% of arable land is left uncultivated in most years – quite an irony considering that the homelands have too many people on too little land.

In Ciskei, over 90% of the average household income is derived from nonagricultural sources. Yet the perception persists that the homelands still offer a viable occupation for blacks in farming as opposed to their becoming integrated into the industrial economy of South Africa.

In general, turnover in the livestock industry in the homelands is low. In Transkei, for example, the annual 'offtake' of cattle is only 5% as against 20-25% in commercial farming in 'white' South Africa. A rise in 'offtake' is desirable, since the current number of cattle in Transkei is double what it should be for long-term sustained productivity. A similar situation prevails in KwaZulu. Between 1957 and 1973, for every animal that was sold or slaughtered, two died on average of natural causes.

Overstocking and consequent soil erosion are inevitable, given the overcrowding of the homelands. Moreover, cattle are traditionally seen as social security, not as productive assets. There is a great deal of wealth locked up in the herd. The national KwaZulu herd of 1,7 million cattle is worth slightly more than the whole of the homeland's sugar industry in capital value.

The need to conserve soil through sustainable agricultural systems is not appreciated by the majority of the homeland population. Their needs are immediate. A hungry stomach cannot accommodate a long-term view on natural resource management.

Furthermore, cattle ownership even in the current situation of overstocking represents rational economic behaviour as it provides the highest rate of return available. The return arises from the use of cattle as draught animals. Ploughing with a team of two oxen, as opposed to hoeing, enables a family to cultivate seven times as much land where this is available.

Although the homelands could meet their own food needs in the next decade, the realization of this potential will require radical changes in agricultural practice. Further capital investment in farms and distribution networks will be needed. Moreover, a leap in agricultural productivity is out of the question while the homelands are maintained as overcrowded dormitories for 'white' industries. A reservoir of able-bodied men must remain at home to tend the farms. For the landless, however, the only salvation will be to multiply the job opportunities in the other sectors of the economy. This calls for training and development, easier access to capital and the sweeping away of all obstructions to opening up small service and manufacturing businesses.

White farming – a different world
The situation of the white commercial farming sector is strikingly different. Just over 85 million hectares of farmland are occupied by South Africa's 50 000 white farming families. A quarter of these farmers account for three-quarters of the total agricultural output. They are as advanced in their farming methods as any farmers in the world, and are an example for the rest of South Africa to follow.

Agricultural productivity in 'white' areas is largely governed by climatic and weather factors. It is estimated that on average about

---

COMMERCIAL AGRICULTURE

 ✳ **Contributes 6% of GDP, down from 21% in 1911**
 ✳ **Occupies 85% of South Africa's agricultural land**
 ✳ **23% of production lost annually due to weather**
 ✳ **Declining rate of increase in food production**
but
    SA's food needs can be met by:
 ✳ **Increased maize and wheat yields on less land**
 ✳ **Improved animal husbandry and 'turnover' rates**

Chart 28

23% of agricultural production is lost annually on account of adverse weather conditions which include drought, excessively high temperatures, hail and frost.

Although it is well known that South Africa has distinct cycles of above and below average rainfall, and that most of the country receives less than 500 mm of rainfall per annum, dry spells are traditionally described as 'droughts'. Substantial drought aid is paid to farmers in so-called 'drought-stricken' areas. During the 30-year period to 1985, 27% of the country was 'drought-stricken' for more than 50% of the time. It is, therefore, a moot point whether such areas are suitable for farming at all.

Because of the depopulation of white rural areas, there is no land pressure in 'white' South Africa. However, loss of land to nonagricultural activities will continue to reduce the amount of available arable land. The annual loss of agricultural land to competing uses varies between 30 000 and 70 000 hectares. In the eastern Transvaal Highveld, 200 000 hectares of high-potential agricultural land are already being used or are earmarked for mining activities.

Two myths debunked

Two myths pervade thinking on land availability and use in South Africa: firstly, that the homelands include a major portion of the region's high-potential arable land and, secondly, that blacks are inherently incompetent farmers. The first suggestion is easily refuted by the statistics quoted above, which demonstrate that the homelands have the same proportion of arable land to total farmland (15%) as does 'white' South Africa.

The second assertion ignores the success of black agriculture in the eastern Cape and the western Transvaal in the second half of the 19th century, before the introduction of a wide range of legislation that crippled black agriculture. The Glen Grey Act of 1894, which restricted black farmers to ten acres each, started the rot. Subsequent discriminatory legislation prejudiced any likelihood of fair competition between black and white farmers. Still, critics will contend that this does not explain the deplorable farming standards in much of Africa. The answer is that the African continent is riddled with too much state intervention. Moreover, population growth and the resulting pressure on resources has limited the capacity of most African countries to take advantage of modern capital-intensive farming techniques.

We certainly do not advocate that the whole of South Africa be turned into a patchwork of small subsistence farms. The plea is for equal opportunity for all South Africans to farm in the most efficient manner possible.

Self-sufficiency in food

The agricultural sector contributes about 6% of South Africa's GDP. An area of about 1,2 million hectares of land is currently irrigated and a further 256 000 hectares are thought to have potential. An estimated 25-30% of the gross national agricultural product is derived from irrigated lands.

The annual rate of increase in food production in South Africa dropped from 7% in the 1960s to 3,1% in the 1970s. The Institute for Futures Research at Stellenbosch estimates that the rate of increase for the period 1980-2000 will be 2,4% per annum. Notwithstanding the relatively low yields of field crops in South Africa, there is good reason to believe that commercial agriculture will adequately provide for the country's food needs well into the 21st century. If recent rainfall patterns hold, the early 1990s should provide a substantial increase in food production before the lean dry years of the turn of the century arrive.

The area under individual crops varies substantially from year to year, but currently 4 million hectares are planted to maize, 1,9 million hectares to wheat and 0,4 million hectares to sugar cane – the three main crops of the commercial farming sector. These together contribute a little over 60% to the total income from field crops.

Although maize yields from the commercial farming sector are very low by world standards (2,0 tonnes/hectare versus 3,6 tonnes/hectare), the national need of 6-8 million tonnes per annum is well within potential supply. Wheat yields are also low (0,9 tonnes/hectare in South Africa versus a global average of 2,3 tonnes/hectare), but the total crop can be expected to increase by 4% per annum from its 1985 level of 2,1 million tonnes to 3,8 million tonnes by the year 2000.

If the 1988-89 season is a measure of things to come, the prospects for the moist 1990s are good. The maize crop was over 10 million tonnes

(30% up on the previous season) and the wheat crop reached a record 3,3 million tonnes.

Estimates put South Africa's total livestock population at 29 million sheep and goats, and 8 million cattle. The numbers of sheep and goats peaked at around 40 million in 1933, then dropped to 24 million in 1946 before rising to the current number.

Under a favourable scenario, demand for red meat would need the current livestock population to increase by 60% by the turn of the century unless there is great improvement in animal husbandry systems. For this reason, pasture upgrading and more frequent 'turnover' of animals must play a key role. The land available for pasture production in South Africa is vast at nearly 84 million hectares. About 13 million hectares are suited to the total replacement of the natural vegetation with planted pastures, and 24 million hectares to reinforcement techniques whereby legumes and selected grass species are introduced. To date two million hectares of improved pasture have been established.

Potential doubling of timber demand
South Africa's indigenous forest resources are extremely limited, both in area and in quality of timber. As a consequence, extensive plantations of pines and eucalypts have been established to meet the demands of the pulp and paper, construction and mining industries. Today, more than 1,2 million hectares are afforested, with the major plantations in the Transvaal (52% of the total) and Natal (36%). The forests currently supply 18 million cubic metres of timber, of which 53% goes to pulp and paper, 23% to sawn timber and 20% to the mining industry.

At present, the national demand for forestry products is increasing at about 3% per annum, and will double by the year 2013. The rate of afforestation is currently in the region of 30 000 hectares per year, still far short of the 40 000 hectares per year needed to meet production goals for the early 21st century. Even when expanded, the area of plantations will be limited to a total of approximately 1,5 million hectares by ecological conditions, legislation to protect water catchments and land prices. Improved genetic types, better forest management and more efficient use of timber will help to meet rising demand, but the shortfall of timber for housing construction and for pulp and paper being experienced at present will be particularly acute in the period between 2000 and 2010. The trees to meet the timber needs of the next two decades are already in the ground.

MISMATCH OF INDUSTRIAL GROWTH POINTS AND WATER AVAILABILITY

Gold, South Africa's primary mineral resource and foreign exchange earner, is concentrated on the high plateau of the country's interior. The development of industry, commerce and human settlement has therefore taken place far from the coast. Almost 60% of South Africa's GDP is produced within the Pretoria-Witwatersrand-Vereeniging (PWV) complex in the Transvaal. Some 42% of the country's urban population lives there. Moreover, the number of people living in the PWV area will increase from 5,9 million in 1985 to 8,5 million in the year 2000.

Water is the most critical resource for any socioeconomic development. However, the rivers of the Vaal River catchment, which drain the PWV complex, produce a mere 4 300 million cubic metres per annum – 8% of the country's total water runoff.

The combined annual runoff of South Africa's rivers is estimated to average 53 500 million cubic metres. On a per capita basis, this is but

---

ECONOMIC GROWTH AND WATER AVAILABILITY

* 59% of South Africa's GDP comes from PWV
* 42% of urban population in PWV
* Vaal catchment provides only 8% of mean annual runoff
* 50% of mean annual runoff already captured in dams
* Total runoff of plateau already captured
* One dam per annum lost to siltation

Chart 29

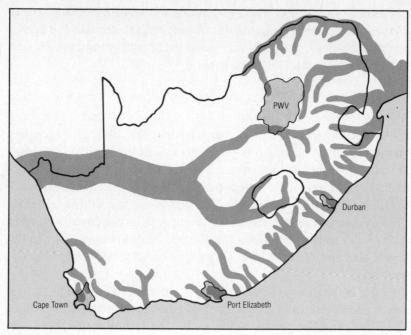

Chart 30 · Distribution of mining and industrial growth points in South Africa relative to water availability (Source: Department of Water Affairs 1986)

19% of the global average. In some areas rivers can have ten consecutive years of less than average flow. Because of this variability and the high evaporation losses from storage, it is estimated that only 62% of the mean annual runoff of South Africa's rivers can be exploited economically.

Existing major dams in South Africa have a total capacity equivalent to 50% of the total mean annual runoff. These dams command virtually the total runoff from the interior plateau. As water availability is distributed poorly in relation to the country's key economic growth points, the cost of providing water in South Africa will continue to rise sharply. Every year it will have to be transported over greater distances to areas of increasing demand.

Exacerbating the problem are poor veld management practices which lead to high levels of soil erosion and sedimentation. These factors cause the loss of 130 million cubic metres of storage capacity, nearly equal to one medium-sized dam such as Midmar or Hartbeespoort, per year. The cost of constructing new dams to replace storage capacity lost to siltation is estimated at between R100 and R200 million per annum.

Total water use in 1980 was 16 000 million cubic metres. Demand is expected to increase to 19 000 million cubic metres in 1990 and 22 000 million cubic metres in the year 2000. To meet this increased demand, expenditure on supply must grow by an average of 8% per annum in real terms and by as much as 16,5% per annum in the short term. In contrast, for the period 1970 to 1985, there was an 8% per annum real decline in expenditure on new dams.

Although half of the developed water resources goes to irrigation, this use is highly cost-inefficient. Water supply to farmers in government irrigation schemes is heavily subsidized. Because of the competing demands for water, and the very high capital costs of such schemes, the development of further large government irrigation projects is being held in abeyance. Most of the recent expansion of irrigation farming has involved private schemes.

The economic return on water use varies widely. In respect of the Vaal River catchment, preliminary calculations show that water use in mining generates 58 times more gross geographic product than water use in agriculture, forestry and fisheries. The equivalent multiples for manufacturing and electricity production, compared to agriculture, are 39 and 19 times respectively.

With the development of the R4 000 million Lesotho Highlands Water Project and the careful management of existing supplies, industrial development in the PWV should be able to proceed to the end of this century without severe constraints.

COAL, ENERGY AND ATMOSPHERIC POLLUTION

South Africa possesses recoverable coal reserves exceeding 58 000 million tonnes or approximately 3% of the global total. These are sufficient to meet local and export requirements well beyond the end of the next century. Coal provides 76% of South Africa's primary energy needs, followed by oil (16%), biomass (6%) and nuclear sources (2%). Sasol and Mossgas should together be able to supply some 40% of South Africa's liquid fuel needs in the early 1990s.

COAL, ENERGY AND AIR POLLUTION

* 80% of South Africa's electricity produced in ETH
* ETH has one of world's worst dispersal climatologies
* ETH emissions total 125 million tonnes per year
* Most emissions from ETH power stations
* 30 to 40 tonnes SO_2 emitted per km^2 per year within ETH
* ETH rainfall acidity equivalent to north-east USA and Europe
* 50% of SA's high-production arable land and forestry resources within ETH

Chart 31

Electricity production in South Africa increased by 8% per annum from 1975 to 1985, while demand increased by 6% per annum, doubling every 12 years. About 80% of South Africa's electricity is produced in the eastern Transvaal Highveld (ETH). For the future, planned growth in production has been considerably cut back by the Electricity Supply Commission (Eskom) in line with lower projections of electricity demand.

The concentration of South Africa's coal reserves and electricity generation in the ETH brings with it serious environmental problems. Because of local meteorological conditions and topographical features, air pollutants are very poorly dispersed over most parts of South Africa. The dispersal climatology of the ETH, in particular, ranks with the most unfavourable anywhere in the world. It is therefore not surprising that air pollution is a matter of growing concern in this region, aptly described as the powerhouse of Africa.

Around 65 million tonnes of coal are burnt annually by our massive power stations, more than 50 million tonnes of this in the ETH. For every tonne of coal that is burnt, approximately two tonnes of carbon dioxide is released. Annual emissions of air pollutants such as particulates, sulphur dioxide, nitrous oxides, carbon dioxide, carbon monoxide and hydrocarbons currently exceed 125 million tonnes over the

ETH. Carbon dioxide accounts for more than 98% of this total. Most of these pollutants come from power stations, but substantial contributions also arise from various smaller industries, discard coal dumps, domestic consumption and motor vehicles. Within the 3 million hectare area of the ETH the sulphur dioxide emission densities – at 30-40 tonnes of SO_2 per square kilometre per year – are as great as the worst conditions found in the north-eastern USA and Europe.

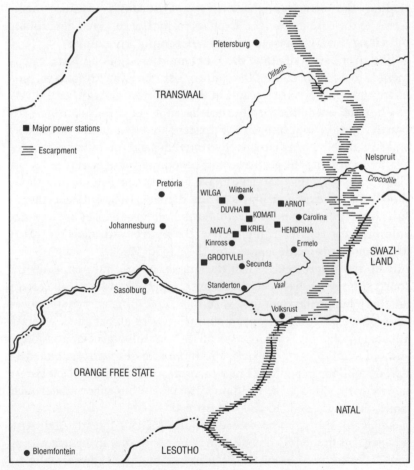

Chart 32 · Eastern Transvaal Highveld: powerhouse of Africa

Rainfall acidity, popularly referred to as 'acid rain', is similar in the ETH to that in north-eastern USA and Europe. This implies that the environment is at high risk in the medium to long term. Over half of South Africa's high-potential agricultural land and half of its forest resources are concentrated in the ETH. The potential economic ramifications are thus obvious.

While the effect of acid rain on cultivated agricultural soils is expected to be insignificant because they are routinely limed, the impact on the strongly acidic soils occupied by natural vegetation might be substantial. But changes might take several decades to manifest themselves to the casual observer. Even scientifically gathered data could, for a long time, be open to several different interpretations.

The river basins draining the ETH and the adjoining Natal catchments provide up to 25% of the country's surface water resources. Sulphate concentrations of streams in the ETH have already been affected, but the economic significance has not yet been quantified. In North America and Europe the impact of acid rain on the life of lakes and streams has been dramatic, leaving thousands of water bodies lifeless and reducing the aesthetic and economic value of vast areas. In Canada, for example, 140 lakes have lost all their fish life and thousands more are experiencing biological damage. In Scandinavia the results have been even more severe. Several thousand lakes are now devoid of sensitive aquatic life such as the insects and snails on which fishes and birds are dependent for their food needs.

Even more spectacular than the impact of acid rain on water resources, however, has been the extensive dieback of forests in certain northern hemisphere countries. In 1986, an estimated 7 million hectares of forests in 15 European countries were classified as severely affected by chemical pollution. A further 22 million hectares of forest showed symptoms of dieback. Production losses were estimated at R2 000 million per annum. The weakening of trees in the Black Forest in Germany was a slow, insidious process – but when the crunch came, death was sudden and widespread.

As noted above, some 50% of South Africa's forestry industry, which earns in total R7 000 million per annum, lies in an area potentially affected by pollution from the emissions of ETH power stations. Although no direct impact of pollution on forest-tree health has yet been demonstrated in the region, experience from other countries should be sufficiently dramatic to alert us to the potential threats to our own forestry industry.

Thus far, there is no firm evidence to prove that human health has been affected by atmospheric pollution in the ETH. But the useful service life of unprotected metals, such as fencing lines and corrugated iron roofs, has been halved in parts of the region. It is unrealistic to assume that the human body will remain unaffected by atmospheric pollution in the ETH.

Although more than R500 million has already been spent on measures to control atmospheric pollution in the ETH, these are considered inadequate to reduce the levels of acid rain in the long term. Tall stacks have helped to disperse gaseous pollutants such as sulphur dioxide more widely, but the costs of removing sulphur from flue gases are exorbitant. The capital outlay for the desulphurization of a single 3 600 MW power station would exceed R500 million, with an additional R100 million in annual running costs. Such investments will have to be weighed against the environmental benefits derived from their implementation. Hence, atmospheric pollution may well worsen until new economically acceptable technologies are developed to control it. Careful monitoring of human health is required.

Nuclear energy is frequently advocated as the clean alternative to coal for South Africa's energy future. At present 15% of the world's electricity, and 2% of South Africa's, is produced from nuclear sources. Ninety per cent of all nuclear electricity is produced in the industrialized countries of the northern hemisphere.

Initially, growth in nuclear power stations was phenomenal, rising from a world total of 80 operational reactors in 1970 to 345 in 1985. Installed electricity-generating capacity using nuclear fuel grew fourteenfold in the same period. But the Three Mile Island and Chernobyl accidents provoked massive resistance to the development of any further nuclear power stations. Growth has all but stopped since the early 1980s, meaning that the proportional contribution of nuclear electricity to global power consumption is almost certain to be less in the year 2000 than it is today.

Despite the near-hysteria generated by the media following Chernobyl, only 31 workers died as a consequence of the accident within the first year. The long-term health impacts of Chernobyl have been the subject of numerous studies. The US Department of Energy projects 28 000 additional fatal cancers in the northern hemisphere over the next 50 years as a consequence of Chernobyl. Alarming though this figure might appear, it amounts to an increased risk of 0,005%. Even within a 30-kilometre radius of Chernobyl, the increased risk is 2%. Furthermore, France, with the highest per capita nuclear energy production level in the world, has not had a single fatal accident in 30 years.

An evaluation of the relative risks to human health of coal-based versus nuclear-based electricity would probably show that, in the long term, nuclear sources are more benign. So we should not dismiss nuclear power from the energy agenda of the future, even though South Africa will not expand its current capacity before the next century. Furthermore, nuclear power is becoming more attractive through the new generation of smaller and safer reactors currently being developed. Japan plans to have 400-600 MW plants operational within 30 years, and plants small enough to operate within industrial areas will follow.

The ultimate goal is for the development of fusion power, a nuclear source free of the dangers inherent in current fission technology. But fusion power is still far off, even if the latest reports about 'cold fusion' are verified. According to the Atomic Energy Corporation's Wynand de Villiers, "the only constant in the fusion scenario is that enthusiasts are still saying that the lead time to get a commercial fusion reactor going is 20 years – exactly what they were saying 20 years ago".

RESTRICTED ACCESS TO ELECTRICITY AND WATER

Of the total energy produced in South Africa, 46% is used in industry, 28% in transport, 10% in households, 9% in mining and 7% in agriculture. South Africa consumes significantly more energy relative to the size of its economy than any other country at a comparable stage of development. Our electricity is amongst the cheapest in the world, but our gas amongst the most expensive.

Today Eskom ranks among the top seven electricity suppliers in the world. It produces approximately 60% of Africa's electricity. Yet the overwhelming majority of South Africa's black population has no access to the electricity grid which serves mainly the 'white' urban areas and farms. Eskom is trying to remedy this situation, but the recent introduction of electricity to Soweto revealed the considerable practical difficulties associated with providing large numbers of low-income families with an electricity network and administering it.

Over 12 million people in the rural and rapidly urbanizing areas use fuel wood as their primary energy source, consuming more than 7,2 million cubic metres of fuel wood per annum. Energy policy in South Africa has concentrated almost exclusively on commercial fuels such as coal, gas, petroleum and electricity for the industrial and metropolitan centres. It has neglected renewable energy resources such as fuel wood and agricultural residues. The needs of underdeveloped areas, both urban and rural, have therefore been overlooked.

In Cape Town, for example, fuel for cooking, heating and lighting often costs more per unit of energy for the poor than it does for those who are better off. Consequently, households without electricity in the poorer suburbs spend more in absolute terms on energy each month than white, middle-class families living in electrified homes.

DOMESTIC ENERGY AND WATER USE

* **Eskom produces 60% of Africa's electricity**
* **70% of SA's population excluded from Eskom network**
* **Over 12 million people use fuel wood as primary energy source**
* **Cost of domestic energy is highest among poor**
* **Energy policy has focused on commercial fuels**
* **No shortage of energy, only inequitable distribution**
* **Access to water differs considerably between First and Third World communities**
* **Water consumption of urban blacks is 10% that of urban whites**

Chart 33

In KwaZulu, fuel wood consumption is about 2,8 million cubic metres per year, taking 75 000 man (woman!) years to collect. If wood gathering is counted as part of food preparation, then more effort is put into the preparation of food than into growing it.

Indigenous woodlands can provide about half of KwaZulu's current needs without harmful effects and without transporting wood over long distances. This leaves a shortfall of 1,4 million cubic metres a year. To provide this on a sustained yield basis will require about 125 000 hectares of small fuel wood plantations or 'woodlots'. This is about 100 times the existing area of woodlots in KwaZulu and is clearly an unattainable goal.

However, there is no overall shortage of energy in South Africa. The prime short-term goal must be to widen the distribution of electricity throughout black areas and to work out, in consultation with leaders of the local communities, practical systems of charging the consumer. No matter how well conceived, no system will work unless there is significant economic growth within these communities to enable them to pay for energy at nonsubsidized rates. However, the problem is not insurmountable in terms of national resources. The electrification of the country's major black towns, including power generation, would cost in the order of R6 000 million, considerably less than today's cost of one synthetic-fuel plant such as Sasol II.

In addition to the problem of electrification, a huge disparity exists in the distribution of water between First and Third World communities. Again, we present a few examples to demonstrate the dimension of a problem that is unlikely to change significantly within the next decade.

Consumption of water within the Ciskei averages 9 litres per person per day, compared with the World Health Organization's goal of 50 litres. In the smaller towns of the eastern Cape Province, per capita consumption by blacks is 19 litres, and in the metropolitan area of Port Elizabeth it is 80 litres, against the white average of 200 litres per day.

In middle-class, metropolitan, predominantly white homes, an average of two or three taps per inhabitant is not unusual. In the Mhala district of Gazankulu in the eastern Transvaal, by contrast, the average works out at one tap for no fewer than 760 people.

Not only quantity, but also quality of water is crucial for life – or death. At present, 5 out of every 100 children in rural areas die before the age of five from diseases caused by contaminated water.

Again, the problem will not be resolved solely by an ambitious government aid programme to universalize the distribution of drinking water. It is a matter of uplifting the deprived communities through education and training, and bringing them into the mainstream of the economy. Only then will it be possible to provide long-term, affordable answers to local water shortages without distorting the economy as a whole.

LIMITS TO GROWTH IN THE MARINE ENVIRONMENT

South Africa has three major oceanic systems abutting it. To the south, the wide expanse of the Southern Ocean controls the South African climate and weather, as well as influencing the climate of the whole planet. To the east is the Indian Ocean, with its warm Agulhas Current that washes the country's southern and eastern coasts. The South Atlantic Ocean lies off the country's western seaboard. Its Benguela Current, with vast areas of cold upwelled water, underpins South Africa's valuable fishing industry.

Currently, the total annual catch of the world's marine fisheries is some 80 million tonnes. Our local industry holds twenty-second position with a catch of approximately 600 000 tonnes. It earns revenue of some R800 million a year, based on resources that are almost fully exploited. Since there are few alternatives close to the coast, the industry will have to fish further afield and deeper if it is to grow in future.

Prospects for the expansion of the country's maricultural industry (producing mainly shellfish at present) are limited. Areas sheltered from the high-energy surf zone (a feature of much of South Africa's coast) are scarce. More hopeful, however, is the future of marine mining operations, involving mainly diamonds, petroleum oil, gas and heavy minerals.

Unlike most industrialized nations, South Africa's industries are not clustered around its coast – at harbours, in bays or at river mouths. As touched upon already, this peculiarity stems from the fact that most of the deposits of the subcontinent's important minerals occur inland. The severe pollution that besets the coasts of many industrialized nations is, therefore, absent or relatively weak around the South African coast.

Nevertheless, the coastal zone, largely unspoilt until the boom years of the 1960s, has been exploited for tourism and recreation – almost without control. Furthermore, the growth of service industries and the increasing settlement of people along the coast have compounded the damage that is occurring. Rising prosperity would make further demands on the coastal zone for recreation and tourism. A popular statistic reveals that if everyone in South Africa were to stand on the shore simultaneously, there would be less than ten centimetres of coastline per person!

CHANGING BLACK CONSUMPTION PATTERNS

Consumption patterns are in a constant state of flux. They are, therefore, poor indicators of future trends, but they do provide an idea of a nation's socioeconomic profile. We will examine some of them as background to the scenarios developed later. In particular, the changing patterns of consumer spending among the black population will alter future demand for resources.

Major structural changes have occurred in the South African economy over the past 70 years. Agriculture has dropped from 21% of GDP in 1911 to 6% today, a trend repeated in all developed economies. Mining has slipped from 28% to 14%, whereas manufacturing has increased from 4% to 23%. Trade, catering and financial services have increased from 23% of GDP in 1946 to 27% now, and current government spending from 10% to 19% in the same period.

The trend away from agriculture and mining – towards manufacturing, construction and services – is expected to continue. Whether government expenditure increases or decreases as a percentage of total GDP in the future, however, will very much depend on which one of our socioeconomic scenarios comes into play.

A significant contribution to the growth of the South African economy in the 1980s has been the rise of the informal sector. Informal markets are particularly evident in urban areas, since job opportunities in the formal sector and in the rural subsistence economy have failed to keep pace with the huge number of new work seekers. The estimate of what the informal sector adds to national GDP is officially put at

ECONOMIC GROWTH AND CONSUMPTION PATTERNS

✻ To maintain per capita income, GDP must grow at
2,4% per year
✻ To accommodate the labour force, 5,4% GDP growth
per year required
✻ To uproot poverty, 10% GDP growth per year required
✻ In 1985, personal disposable income of blacks R973
per year versus R8 326 for whites
✻ White consumption patterns will remain constant but
blacks' will continue to change
✻ Under favourable scenario, sharpest increases in
housing, transport, education and insurance
✻ Strength of the informal sector

Chart 34

3%. However, academic sources think the figure lies somewhere between 20% and 40%. The wide range in estimates is probably due to lack of a clear definition of what constitutes formal and informal business.

The taxi industry is a potent example of what can be achieved when combining the 'high-tech' strengths of big business with the entrepreneurial drive of the small-business and informal sectors. It is now worth some R3 000 million in taxis alone and has in four years provided jobs, directly or indirectly, for 300 000 people. The last figure is equivalent to 60% of the work force of the entire gold mining industry. These jobs have been created out of thin air with no government support! The taxi industry has proved that blacks are every inch the entrepreneurs that whites are. This economic miracle was a direct result of an inflexible public transport system. The black taxi owners spotted the gap – and exploited it.

The retail and construction industries will probably be the next to follow this innovative lead. Whether it is informal hawkers teaming up with formal wholesalers, or small black builders getting together with large construction companies, this new wave of activity which

73

epitomizes a dual-logic economy is unstoppable. Already 'spazas' – back-room shops in black townships – account for R3 000 million per annum of sales in grocery goods.

In order to maintain the status quo in per capita income, GDP will have to grow at 2,4% per annum – equivalent to the population growth rate. An annual economic growth rate of 5,4% would be needed to accommodate new work seekers in the formal-sector economy. However, the rate would have to be consistently close to 10% per annum in the 1990s in order to "uproot poverty", in the words of Francis Wilson and Mamphela Ramphele.

Consumption patterns are determined by the level of personal disposable income (personal income less personal taxes) within each socioeconomic group. In 1985, the personal disposable income for blacks was calculated at R973 per annum per head versus R8 326 for whites. In the same year, the average Household Subsistence Level (HSL) for black households (six persons) was R4 080, or R680 per person. While black household incomes were on average above the HSL, the skewed distribution of incomes meant that more than 50% of black households lived below the HSL.

Given the difference in per capita income levels, spending patterns differ markedly between the black and white communities. Out of every rand blacks spend on consumer goods and services, 38 cents is spent on food, 11 cents on clothing and footwear and 9 cents on alcoholic beverages – proportionately more than twice as much as whites spend on these items. Bearing in mind, however, that whites spend on average 8,5 times more per person than blacks do, white expenditure per person on food, for example, is 3,7 times greater than the black equivalent.

For every rand spent by whites, 21 cents is spent on housing, electricity, fuel and light, 13 cents on transport, and 15 cents on insurance and pension funds – proportionately more than double the amount blacks spend on these items. White expenditure per person on insurance and pension funds is 27 times that of blacks, and in the case of housing, electricity, fuel and light, and transport, 20 times.

White consumption patterns are expected to remain much as they are over the next decade under all but the worst scenarios. Changes, however, can be anticipated among black people. The degree of change will be dependent upon whether there is an across-the-board accumulation of wealth in South Africa or the persistence of poverty. Already the rising affluence of blacks in urban areas is leading to shifts in consumption which are benefiting such industries as lager beer and poultry. National sales of the former are increasing in volume at 8-10% per annum and the latter at 7% per annum.

Overall, one can expect stable growth in demand for such items as food, drink, tobacco, clothing and footwear. But substantial growth will occur in a good scenario for higher-quality foods, luxury goods, cars, houses, household appliances, education, insurance, pension funds and recreation. In this scenario, too, the informal and small business sectors will be the birthplace of the future entrepreneurial stars of big black business. The stock market, pension funds and large commercial banks will provide the crucial stepping stones, in terms of capital needed, for the transition to be made from local enterprise to national and international business.

6 'Key Uncertainties'

The 'rules of the game' set the framework within which we will paint South Africa's future environmental scenarios. But first, we must examine the 'key uncertainties'.

DISCARDING THE GLOBAL UNCERTAINTIES

In the remaining years of this century, it is unlikely that the two main components of global change – human population and the 'greenhouse effect' – will significantly affect the South African environment. Their impact in the early 21st century is not yet sufficiently clearly understood for scenarios to be developed specifically around them. Furthermore, as the threat of a full-scale nuclear war diminishes in the light of the detente which now exists between the US and the Soviet Union, we will exclude 'nuclear winter', too, from the list of scenario determinants.

Changes to the global environment will undoubtedly affect South Africa in the long term. However, unless some major, unexpected catastrophe occurs, external factors are not as important in shaping our environment as are the 'key uncertainties' under our own control. Obviously, though, South Africa must cooperate with the other nations of the world in preventing the worst outcomes of the 'greenhouse effect' and the depletion of the ozone layer. Moreover, population growth is as much a problem here as in any other developing country. Anything South Africa does to curb its own population growth will contribute towards solving the global problem as well.

REGIONAL 'WILD CARDS'

It is worth mentioning some of the 'wild card' surprises which could dramatically change the course of events in southern Africa. But trying to accommodate these in a multidimensional model of the future is simply not helpful.

The regional impact of AIDS is an unknown quantity at present. The data base is too small to start writing doomsday scenarios for central and southern Africa in which deaths from AIDS outnumber births, causing negative population growth rates. What is clear, though, is that Africa differs from Europe and North America at present. In the latter regions, AIDS is largely confined to high-risk groups such as homosexuals and intravenous drug users. In Africa, AIDS is commonly transmitted heterosexually and there are more cases of mothers passing it on to children than in Europe and North America.

The real danger of the disease is the length of time which elapses between a person being infected by the virus and being diagnosed as sero-positive on the one hand, and becoming a full-blown AIDS victim on the other. Currently, it is thought that this period can extend to ten years. Thus, before the disease becomes overtly spectacular enough to change society's behavioural patterns, it is possible that the pool of sero-positive people will be so large that the spread of the disease will be virtually unstoppable.

If this were to occur, AIDS would be the single most important factor in any scenario exercise. Life would literally revolve around AIDS. A plague mentality would develop. It would have serious antisocial

---

'KEY UNCERTAINTIES'

Global:
* **Population growth**
* **'Greenhouse effect'**
* **'Nuclear winter'**

Regional:
* **AIDS**
* **Rinderpest, malaria, cholera**
* **Angola/Namibia/Mozambique**

Pivotal to SA scenarios:
* **Socioeconomic trajectories**
* **Environmental management**

Chart 35

repercussions, as healthy people attempted to isolate themselves completely from those diagnosed as sero-positive or stricken with the advanced form of the disease.

No cure or vaccine is yet in sight to combat AIDS, but breakthroughs cannot be ruled out. In the meantime, it is essential that saturation coverage in the media is given throughout the subcontinent to the nature of AIDS and ways in which the risks of contracting it can be lowered.

Other diseases which could seriously affect South Africa are malaria, hepatitis-B, cholera, bilharzia, foot-and-mouth disease and rinderpest. These are just a few of the host of tropical diseases which are either present in South Africa, or capable of being introduced from neighbouring states. The incidence of these diseases could be increased dramatically in the 21st century if global warming occurs. People forget at their peril that Africa, more than any other continent, represents a fragile balance between nature and civilization. Destroy civilization, and nature swiftly reasserts itself.

On the political front, critical factors will be the kinds of government that evolve in Angola, Mozambique and Namibia, and the level of regional cooperation. Political stability or instability in the surrounding states will have a major bearing on South Africa's own future. In a rosy scenario, one can envisage a regional 'common market' where South Africa imports its oil from Angola and some of its food and timber from Zimbabwe, Swaziland and Mozambique. In return, South Africa would export manufactured goods such as cars, spares and industrial plant and equipment to these states, as well as providing them with technical and financial services.

In a downside scenario of war in the region, the borders between South Africa and the surrounding states may easily be closed. This will do untold harm to the countries that rely on South Africa's transport system for exports and imports. No amount of foreign aid will offset the damage to their economies.

In the immediate future, the outcome of the settlement in Namibia and the actions of its first elected government will have a critical bearing on the course of South Africa's own affairs. In the eyes of many white people here, Namibia is a make-or-break example of whether or not negotiation is a practical strategy.

The primary motivation for this study is to examine the environmental consequences of various economic paths that could develop in South Africa during the next decade. Logically, it then follows that there are two pivotal uncertainties, linked with one another, on which the scenarios should be based.

The first is the future political, social and economic course which South Africa will take. The second relates to the way in which the use of environmental resources is managed. This, in turn, depends on the relative importance which the public attaches to the environment in relation to other societal goals.

OPTIONS FOR SOUTH AFRICA'S ECONOMY

In regard to the first uncertainty, we have chosen to use the outputs of Anglo's previous scenario study as inputs to this one. In other words, the 'High Road', 'Low Road' and 'Wasteland' scenarios are 'key uncertainties' in this exercise. Despite their simplicity, these scenarios have fulfilled their original objective: to improve the quality of the debate about South Africa's future by offering a fresh perspective on the choices available to South Africans.

'High Road'

This path assumes that South Africa will build its future on its three greatest strengths:

– Its modern infrastructure of roads, bridges, harbours, railways, electricity system and telecommunication networks, which is an indispensable launch pad for a new phase of economic growth. No other developing country can match South Africa in terms of infrastructure.

– Its treasure-trove of mineral resources, which still puts South Africa among the top nations in the world when measured in terms of the value of mineral reserves per head. In addition to exporting these minerals in their raw primary form, South Africa can use them to develop a wide range of secondary industries.

– Its people, who have proven themselves – black and white alike – to be natural and industrious entrepreneurs capable of taking on the best in the world.

'HIGH ROAD'

✳ **Negotiated political settlement**
✳ **Multiparty political system**
✳ **Independent judiciary, decentralized power**
✳ **Limited government intervention in economy**
✳ **Government's budget cut in real terms**
✳ **Free-enterprise, dual-logic economy**
✳ **Reversal of sanctions**
✳ **Inflation rate reduced**
✳ **Mass education programme**

Chart 36

However, the 'High Road' cannot materialize unless nine interdependent conditions are met.

First, the process of negotiation and the building of alliances across the colour line, which is already well evident in the economy and is beginning to take hold in the political arena, must continue to spread. We are coming closer to the core of the problem – the sharing of political power – all the time. However, unlike other African states which gained independence from a colonial authority, power in South Africa is being rearranged internally. For this type of transformation to succeed, patience, high economic growth and the maintenance of law and order are prerequisites. All the principal parties, internally and externally, should do everything they can to ensure a smooth evolution with minimal shocks to the system.

Without prejudging the outcome of negotiation, we offer the remaining eight conditions as food for thought.

Second, a multiparty political system should be entrenched in the constitution so that, if a government is corrupt and inefficient, it can be voted out at the polls. Citizens work harder under a clean administration, where graft does not form an invisible tax on honestly earned income.

Third, whatever the ultimate composition of central government, its power must be limited in two ways: by an independent judiciary, and by a constitution that includes a Bill of Rights and devolves many of the important political and economic decisions to regional and local authorities. In the first regard, it can be seen in the Far East that rule of law, respect for civil liberties and individual ownership of property are – more than any other qualities – responsible for high economic growth. Common sense holds that entrepreneurs are more creative and productive in an environment where they feel secure, where individual freedom of choice is maximized and where the assets under their control belong to them.

Regarding a proposed constitution, too many powerful interest groups exist in South Africa for them not to be granted some autonomy. Nevertheless, we are talking of a universal franchise for the country, with checks and balances built into the structure so that no single interest group can dominate all the others. The US Senate, for example, by having equal representation from each state, ensures that large states such as California cannot dominate the small ones. The real issue for South Africa is how to gain democracy without losing it subsequently to a tyrant. The new constitution should be drafted with this constantly in mind.

Fourth, government's intervention in the running of the economy should be focused on setting fiscal and monetary policies. It could also act as a coach to industry and even as referee when it comes to maintaining a competitive environment. Broadly, its role should be analogous to that of game rangers in a game park. The latter are there to provide the best conditions for the wild plants and animals which are the real champions. After all, people go to the Kruger National Park to look at the flora and fauna, not the game rangers! Government must be there to support the wealth creators – not the other way round.

Socialists often quote the examples of South Korea, Taiwan and Japan as economies with heavy government intervention. But they are wrong. Those governments are not antagonistic to industry. They do not commandeer industry; they do not overregulate it. They simply play the role of coach and referee described above.

Fifth, the government's budget in the 1990s should be gradually cut in real terms, which will entail a reduction in the number of civil servants and the streamlining of government departments. Studies have shown that economic growth is positively correlated with lower government expenditure as a percentage of GDP. People perform better if they are taxed less and have fewer bureaucratic constraints.

Sixth, a free-enterprise, dual-logic economy must be allowed to thrive. Deregulation should be implemented down to street level. Employee share ownership schemes ought to be widely instituted to allow greater participation by workers in the wealth-creation process. Big business should subcontract simpler, low-tech activities to small business. The housing shortage in particular could be overcome using this principle. Output of goods and services should be determined by the taste of consumers, not according to quotas ordained from above by central planners. The difficulties associated with the restructuring of both the Soviet and Chinese economies make it plain that free enterprise is like pregnancy. Neither condition can be a half measure!

Seventh, sanctions should be reversed and foreign capital in the form of equity and long-term loans must once again flow into South Africa. South African goods must be allowed to compete directly with those of any other nation in any market in the world. If this were the case, South Africa's world market share in many instances would undoubtedly increase because of the quality and competitive pricing of its goods, and its past performance in honouring contracts.

At the same time, the government should foster a favourable environment for new export businesses to be established in South Africa, especially in the field of semimanufactured and manufactured goods and services, where the real added value lies.

Eighth, inflation in South Africa must be brought down to 5% per annum or thereabouts as rapidly as possible. This will not be achieved through wage and price freezes – South America provides the latest example of the failure of these measures – but by addressing the underlying cause of inflation: too much money chasing too few goods.

More open competition in the market place is required in addition to intensive training programmes to develop workers so that their future wage increases will be matched by improvements in productivity.

Only in a low-inflationary environment will people begin to save again, thus providing more money for investment. Moreover, it is only under these conditions that businessmen will have their confidence in the long-term prospects of this country restored. Once this has been achieved, they will be willing to risk capital on new 'greenfields' projects with long payback periods. The turnaround in South Africa's economic fortunes must be led by new investment, not higher consumer spending.

Low inflation is also conducive to greater respect for the environment, as long-term benefits are no longer discounted at rates which render them worthless.

Ninth, South Africa must embark on a mass education programme similar to those in Japan and South Korea. Quality and quantity ought to be targeted together. In respect of the first element, teaching must be made a more attractive profession by paying teachers more, in line with commerce and industry. The only way this can be done without placing further burdens on the shoulder of the taxpayer will be by cutting down the number of administrators per teacher. Japan has one of the finest education systems in the world with the smallest civil service. An added benefit is that greater devolution of power to schools themselves has generally raised the standard of education.

The other essential action regarding quality is to focus the curriculum more on education that is relevant for society's practical needs. One of the best statistics for telling whether a nation is going up or down in the world rankings is the number of engineers per lawyer. Engineers create wealth: lawyers generally do not!

A balance must patently exist between the sciences and the humanities. That is what this book is all about. Nonetheless, the emphasis in this country, particularly in the realm of black education, is still not sufficiently on mathematics, physical sciences, technology or training in job-related skills. It is no coincidence that companies in West Germany and Japan, more than any others in the world, have achieved real worker participation in the management process. For they are the ones with the most highly trained work forces on the shop floor, to whom management decisions can be delegated.

Regarding quantity of education, South Africa is well placed to correct the situation. Given its 'high-tech' base, the country can launch nationwide screen-based education programmes using videos, interactive computer programmes, television and radio. These can be used to improve teaching skills, and make good teachers go further by screening their classes to the country at large. But Eskom will first have to electrify South Africa as a whole.

Education above all gives people self-respect. They do not have to rely on welfare. They are taught to respect the family and community at the same time as they pursue their own interests. Awareness of others and a sense of what is morally right and wrong does not have to be forced or imposed upon them by the state. In short, the 'High Road' begins with a sound education system.

These nine conditions are a tall order for any society to attain, let alone one under such pressure as South Africa. It will need exceptional courage and the development of a common vision which transcends sectional interests and makes of South Africa a winning nation.

Nevertheless, no other option is available if we are to meet the most critical goal of all from an environmental point of view: a slowed rate of population growth. Within the shorter time horizon of this study to the year 2000, only very minor changes in population growth rates can be expected. But the outcome of a 'High Road' scenario will be considerably lower population growth rates as we enter the 21st century. Indeed, without the socioeconomic benefits of the 'High Road', South Africa's black population will never progress through a reasonable demographic transition. The alternative – reversible only by famine, disease or war – is an unbridled growth in numbers to more than 170 million by the end of the 21st century. A population of this size would far exceed South Africa's capacity to meet the resource needs for a high quality of life on a sustained basis.

In terms of this study, therefore, the objective of raising per capita income through new wealth creation is of paramount importance. The goal should be to double national income per head by the turn of the century, which requires an economic growth rate of 8-10% per annum.

In the short term, real income per black person could be adjusted by immediately transferring wealth from the white to the black community. However, in a country where GDP is only about R5 700 a head on average, there is little room to manoeuvre. A marginal improvement in black incomes through redistribution would cause white incomes to fall precipitately. Such action would demotivate whites and probably lead to their exodus. Penal rates of tax and confiscation of property have no place on the 'High Road'. What is needed is a much larger cake, not a sudden change in the way it is cut.

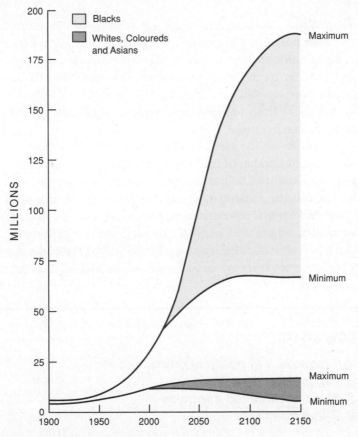

Chart 37 · Projections of South Africa's population growth (Source: President's Council 1983)

It would be remiss, in the shadow of overpopulation, not to mention the critical significance of family planning on the 'High Road'. But it cannot work in isolation. Per capita incomes must be rising at the same time. In China, where a one-child policy has been in practice for several years, the drawbacks of coercive measures of birth control are alarming. Financial inducements and punishments have led to completely unacceptable practices, such as the killing of first-born girls. There is a fine line between persuasion and coercion: it must not be crossed.

'Low Road'

The 'Low Road' scenario represents a stagnation of the reform process, with the possibility of a transfer of power to the right wing. Sanctions will be tightened due to lack of tangible progress and the economy will become increasingly controlled. Government will become bigger and more centralized. State departments will multiply. The exclusion of blacks from top government positions eventually leads to confrontation and conflict.

In the 'Low Road' the annual GDP growth rate will average 2,0% in the 1990s, similar to that of the 1975-1984 decade. This is below population growth and well below the level required to meet employment needs. The resulting unemployment will be a major source of unrest and crime. Additional restrictions on foreign travel will evoke a siege-like mentality, which will reinforce the depressed conditions in the economy. Social responsibility programmes will be slashed as foreign firms continue to disinvest from South Africa and local companies

---

'LOW ROAD'

✻ **Stagnation of political reform process**
✻ **Big government**
✻ **More centralized economy**
✻ **Siege mentality**

Chart 38

draw in their horns in the face of lowered cash flows. Censorship, curfews and crackdowns on black trade unions (which will be weakened anyway by rising unemployment) will be countered by stayaways and consumer boycotts. This scenario provides a springboard for political instability. But no revolution will be possible in the short to medium term due to the overwhelming military might of the government.

The homelands will descend from the swamp of malnutrition into the pit of starvation. The prosanctions lobby will argue that life is so wretched there already that to increase the wretchedness is inconsequential for the victims. How absurd! Who is bold enough to sacrifice other people's lives now for such indeterminate gains in the long term?

'Wasteland'

Although the 'Low Road' trajectory can theoretically continue for several decades, it cannot go on indefinitely. Increasingly punitive sanctions, scientific and cultural isolation and the emigration of leaders in industry, commerce and learning will reduce South Africa to a military fortress, isolated from the rest of the world. Internal unrest and repression will thrive inside the fortress.

In the end, the 'Low Road' will degenerate into a 'Wasteland' as the atrocities mount on all sides. Hatred will become insuperable. The world will wash its hands of South Africa. The so-called frontline states will arm themselves to the teeth in order to counter hot-pursuit operations by South Africa.

Regional conflict and civil war will lead to the final collapse of the economy. The infrastructure will deteriorate beyond repair and even subsistence agriculture will be seriously impaired. The country will be divided into several power blocs, each warlord supported by different international powers according to ideology. While repressive regimes will maintain some order in major cities, the rural areas will fall into chaos. Convoys will be compulsory on the main routes. Refugees will stream to cities and towns which, in turn, become foci of desolation as natural resources of food, fuel wood, shelter and water are exhausted. Wild plants and the animals of national parks and nature reserves will be destroyed.

It is said that the one thing that can be learnt from history is that one does not learn from history. South Africans suffer from the 'ostrich

'WASTELAND'

- **✻ Regional conflict and civil war**
- **✻ Collapse of infrastructure**
- **✻ Flood of refugees to cities**
- **✻ A repeat of Lebanon**

Chart 39

syndrome' – a great reluctance to admit that this country could easily and rapidly descend into the socioeconomic and environmental wasteland exemplified by certain African, south-east Asian and Middle Eastern states. Examples of "an alternative too ghastly to contemplate" – a phrase immortalized by the late John Vorster – have emerged right on our doorstep in the last decade.

The possibility of turning South Africa into a wasteland is denied by both extreme left- and right-wing groups: they believe that transition to straight majority rule, or the maintenance of a white oligarchy, is achievable without environmental cost or economic collapse. It may mean some hardships for those opposed to the ideology of the winning side, but no wasteland. On the contrary, the new society will be a veritable paradise for the winners.

Such visions are both naive and irresponsible. The 'winner takes all' philosophy of some aspirant leaders is a pipe dream. A far more probable outcome is continuous, debilitating strife that precludes anything more than a subsistence economy and ensures a return to deep-seated tribal animosities. The formal agricultural sector and the manufacturing and mining industries will suffer irredeemable damage.

If a socialist regime attains power, the nationalization of all land and the compulsory introduction of cooperatives will wreck productivity and increase poverty in both rural and urban communities. Africa is replete with examples of failed agricultural collectivism. A hungry world is turning its back on socialist agricultural policies.

In the alternative event of a right-wing oligarchy assuming power, a repressive security apparatus will dominate every aspect of existence. George Orwell's *1984* will be the South African reality. Neither option bodes well for the maintenance, let alone the improvement, of the quality of life.

The closest parallel to the 'Wasteland' scenario is the experience of Lebanon. In 1975, Lebanon was one of the wealthiest countries in the Middle East, just as South Africa is one of the richest in Africa today. Little more than a decade later, Lebanon has all but self-destructed. Half of Beirut has been burnt down, but still the shelling continues and car bombs maim and kill innocent civilians going about their daily lives. Yet if one had asked a citizen of Beirut in 1975 to predict what his country would be like today, very few would have mentioned a wasteland.

It does happen – and more quickly than one expects.

ENVIRONMENTAL MANAGEMENT – STRONG OR WEAK

This study focuses on economic growth, quality of life and environmental health as the three interdependent elements which determine the prosperity and wellbeing of individuals and nations. South Africa's future rests on the ability of policy makers and the public to interrelate decisions on the economy, the environment and society. Wise management of any two of these elements, without care for the other, is inadequate for sustained development.

Despite the apparent simplicity of this model, the 20th century has been beset by growing conflicts between the environment and development. In many countries of the world, rapid economic growth has been fuelled by a ruthless pillaging of natural resources. This approach has often generated long-term environmental and socioeconomic problems far more costly to repair than the short-term gains derived.

The 1980s have signalled a growing recognition of the interdependence of environmental health and development. A distinction can be drawn between countries in which the actions of both the public and private sectors are directed towards sustaining environmental health; and those which adopt the *laissez-faire* approach of trusting in technologies of the future to repair any damage done to the environment today.

In short, one can categorize countries into those where a national environmental ethic is present and those where it is absent. The con-

89

trast between a strong and weak environmental ethic is illustrated in chart 40.

In regard to the first pairing mentioned in the tabulation, the Scandinavian countries can take pride in a long tradition of environmental consciousness. Third World countries which are emerging with a good track record include Costa Rica in Central America, Zimbabwe in Africa and Thailand in the Far East. Those which still have a long way to go to achieve the right balance include, among others, the Soviet Union, China, the Eastern European nations and the newly industrialized countries of the Far East.

The second pairing is best illustrated on the positive side by farming practice in Western Europe which, combined with a favourable climate, has permitted centuries of crops to be produced without harm to the farmland; and, on the negative side, by the chopping down of tropical forests which has yielded easy profits in the short term to the countries concerned, but could qualify as a long-term calamity to the world as a whole.

A strong environmental ethic in the third, fourth and fifth pairings requires a change in attitude in corporate boardrooms and government corridors. The environment is no longer an afterthought. On the contrary, from the outset it figures as a key component in deliberations. Moreover, the public are not just lobbied to accept a project – whether it is a new mine, highway, dam or missile testing site. Instead, their opinions are genuinely sought and heeded in the preparatory phase before commitments are made and cancellation is too costly.

The sixth pairing is best illustrated by considering the fate of the elephant and rhinoceros. The underlying cause of the endangerment of these two species is demand for ivory and rhino horn. Demand in consuming countries has to be pared through education and legislation in order to squeeze the profit margin of the trade to a level where the risks of poaching are no longer acceptable. Merely capturing poachers in game parks is not going to solve the problem – there will always be other poachers to take their place as long as the returns are high.

An initial step towards reducing world trade in ivory was taken in June 1989 when the major consumers, Japan and the USA, together with the European Community and several other governments, agreed to ban the imports of both raw and processed ivory from Afri-

ENVIRONMENTAL MANAGEMENT OPTIONS

Strong environmental ethic

✶ Concern for environmental health is balanced against political issues and economic growth

✶ The nation's resources are exploited on a sustainable basis to ensure their long-term profitability.

✶ The environment is an integral part of strategic thinking in companies.

✶ All feasibility studies into major projects incorporate an environmental impact assessment report.

✶ Affected communities are allowed to participate in environmentally sensitive decisions before they are taken.

✶ Early attention is given to the underlying causes of environmental degradation as well as to the symptoms.

✶ Environmental processes are thoroughly researched in order to predict the future consequences of present trends in population and industrial output.

✶ Environmental themes are introduced into appropriate subjects of the school curriculum, and are featured prominently in the mass media and advertising.

✶ Polluters are subject to environmental standards laid down by law, which carry stiff penalties if they are breached.

Weak environmental ethic

✶ Preoccupation with politics and economic growth overshadows all environmental considerations.

✶ Resources are rapidly consumed to maximize immediate profits.

✶ The environment is a 'postscript' in pursuance of business goals.

✶ Development and conservation are viewed as mutually exclusive activities.

✶ Communities are briefed or 'consulted' on projects after the decision to proceed has been taken.

✶ Attention is only focused on the environment when the symptoms are obvious and the damage is usually advanced.

✶ Ad hoc solutions to combat environmental problems are formulated as and when they arise.

✶ The public is environmentally 'illiterate' and easily misled in choices involving the environment.

✶ The taxpayer finances government agencies to clean up environmental pollution after it has occurred.

Chart 40

ca. A similar long-standing ban on the trade in rhino horn has failed simply because the main consumer nations in the Middle and Far East have consistently ignored the ban.

The seventh pairing may well be put to the test with the 'greenhouse effect'. Either nations will take the threat seriously enough to cooperate with one another in pre-empting it; or, if the threat materializes, each nation will be faced with the horrendous task of altering its agricultural structure to suit new weather patterns, and of protecting and moving its coastal communities in the wake of rising sea levels.

In order to spread a strong environmental ethic, schools are the best starting point. It is of no use for government to rely solely on legislation to enforce an ethic. The message of the eighth pairing is that a grass roots approach is the only one that will work in the end. It is the reason why we chose to include the word 'ethic' in the title of this 'key uncertainty', as opposed to 'policy' or 'strategy'. A splendid example of the type of action required is the Southern African Nature Foundation's 'Our Living World' campaign.

The last pairing demonstrates the importance of making the polluter accountable for his actions. He will only stop if it hurts him. The problem with shifting the responsibility onto the shoulders of the taxpayer is that it diffuses the penalty for pollution and ultimately raises the cost for the community as a whole. Littering is a good case in point. Apart from education and easily accessible waste bins, there has to be a fine which hits the pocket of the litterer if he is caught. Otherwise, the municipality is obliged to raise its rates in order to cover the cost of expanding refuse collection.

The principles which underpin a strong environmental management ethic are simple, logical and self-serving. But they differ radically from the policies of the past century. They all demand an element of constraint and presuppose long-term investment horizons. During times of sociopolitical change – and there is no doubt that South Africa must pass through these – the most popular route is one that offers immediate rewards and satisfies immediate needs. But a strong economy in the long run requires the existence of a strong environmental ethic. That means sufficient people who are financially capable of attending to more than the pressing issues of the here and now.

In the coming years, South Africans will have to choose between these two basic approaches. "In the end," says Harvard sociobiologist Edward Wilson, "it will all come down to a decision of ethics — how we value the natural world in which we have evolved and how, increasingly, we regard our status as individuals. We are fundamentally free spirits who reached this high a level of rationality by the perpetual creation of new options." We believe that the best way to ascertain the character of a nation, and gauge its social and environmental health, is to seek out the attitudes of its people to their surroundings. This matters more than race, creed or ideology in the long run.

7 South African Environmental Scenarios

The 'key uncertainties' described in the preceding section, together with the 'rules of the game', shape our environmental scenarios. Since we have treated the 'Wasteland' as a separate option to the 'Low Road' in this exercise rather than as a mere extension of the 'Low Road', six scenarios are possible.

We can immediately rule out two of the scenarios in the matrix on the grounds that strong environmental standards cannot be attained without financial resources and popular commitment – elements which are missing in both the 'Low Road' and 'Wasteland' options. This leaves us with four scenarios which, in ascending order of desirability, we have named 'Paradise Lost', 'Separate Impoverishment', 'Boom and Bust' and 'Rich Heritage'.

We would like to stress again that scenarios are not concerned with exact numbers or outcomes. The uncertainties are too great for that. We are scanning the broad changes in direction that a society can take. Scenarios are no more than simple and consistent stories about the future, illustrating each conceivable direction. We start with the worst scenario and end with the best.

'PARADISE LOST': NO WINNERS, ALL LOSERS

Strongly negative economic growth, massive unemployment, poverty and emigration epitomize 'Paradise Lost'. Unemployment may temporarily be mitigated by the development of large and underemployed work forces within state enterprises and collective farms. Nevertheless, there will still be a remnant of unemployed which resorts to crime and black-market activities.

Initially, the rising frequency of bloody skirmishes will precipitate the rapid depopulation of white rural areas and the abandonment of farms. As the civil war intensifies, refugees will move from affected areas to cities or establish temporary settlements along main roads. Agricultural production will plummet, leading to millions being dependent on food aid. Subsistence economies will spring up in both

Socioeconomic trajectory	Environmental management	
	STRONG	WEAK
HIGH ROAD	RICH HERITAGE	BOOM AND BUST
LOW ROAD	—	SEPARATE IMPOVERISH-MENT
WASTELAND	—	PARADISE LOST

Chart 41 · South African environmental scenarios

rural and peri-urban areas, with a depletion in local resources of arable land, fuel wood and indigenous foods.

An ironic benefit to the environment will be the general breakdown of services. Sabotage of power stations, dams and other major components of the infrastructure will reduce energy generation and distribution – with a corresponding fall in the level of atmospheric pollution. The environmental gain will be insignificant, however, compared to the enormous cost to humanity inherent in this scenario.

Collapse in the standard of living
The impact of 'Paradise Lost' will be particularly dramatic in the urban situation. The large influx of refugees from the rural areas will produce an exponential growth of squatter settlements and an increase in abject poverty. The uncontrolled infiltration of squatters into commercial and affluent residential areas will lead to a rapid increase in the crime rate and vandalization of public and private property. Nothing and no-one will be safe.

Shortages of skilled technicians will severely restrict maintenance of the infrastructure. This will cause the disruption or complete failure of the water supply to industrial and urban domestic users. The for-

'PARADISE LOST'

✳ **"An alternative too ghastly to contemplate"**
✳ **Breakdown of security, law and order**
✳ **Rural depopulation, influx into cities of refugees, emigration of skilled people from SA**
✳ **Collapse of investment and national economy**
✳ **Negative GDP growth**
✳ **Destruction of infrastructure**
✳ **Localized plunder of natural resources**

Chart 42

mal economy and First World life style will suffer abysmal deterioration. The provision of water, fuel and sanitation for urban slums will be utterly inadequate. Not only will water supplies be scarce: where there is water, it will be wasted. (The streets of innumerable cities in Africa are frequently awash from broken pipes.) Health risks will rapidly increase as a consequence of this and inadequate refuse collection. Littering will diminish on account of the absence of disposable containers, paper and plastics. But where organized cleaning services are stopped, waste heaps will foul sidewalks and vacant lots.

Poor sanitation and health services will allow the spread of epidemic diseases which will affect not only the squatter settlements, but also the isolated, affluent minority. Disease has no respect for social status or wealth in conditions of anarchy.

Initially, increased dependence on coal may raise levels of urban smog; but as the transport infrastructure crumbles and energy distribution slows, so too will the rate of coal use decline. All fuel wood reserves will be quickly depleted. Ultimately trees in suburban gardens, parks and other public areas will be cut down. The dearth of fuel wood will cause its price to rise rapidly; its purchase will possibly consume up to half of household expenditure in urban areas far from the resource base. Around the rural settlements along the highways, areas may be totally denuded of trees, with consequent erosion and reduction of fodder and shelter for animals.

Luxury and imported goods and services will disappear from the market. Simply procuring basic essentials such as grain foods, sugar and oil will become a major daily preoccupation. A barter economy will prevail along with a black-market system for the purchase of 'luxury' items such as toiletries, clothing, footwear and paraffin. Petty corruption in the distribution of local goods and foreign-aid supplies will proliferate. Corruption and survival become synonymous in an economy devoid of opportunities to make an honest living.

In the rural areas, the situation will go from bad to worse. Even so, relative to the devastation of the urban areas, the change from an already poor quality of life will be less brutal. Some habitats, such as wetlands and coastal forests, may come under greatly increased pressure. Small farmers will return to shifting cultivation systems to compensate for the lack of artificial fertilizers. But these methods will

---

ENVIRONMENTAL CONSEQUENCES OF 'PARADISE LOST'

Positive
* Cessation of agricultural development
* Recovery of abandoned farmlands
* Reduced industrial pollution

Negative
* Development of inadequately serviced refugee camps: contaminated water, open sewers, litter
* Fuel wood crisis and deforestation
* Declining occupational safety standards
* Crime, corruption, vandalism
* Local foci of soil erosion, extinction of 'muti' plants and animals
* Collapse of national parks
* Misuse of pesticides
* Toxic waste dumping
* Foreign exploitation of marine resources

Chart 43

swiftly exhaust the soil nutrients. The enforcement of any soil conservation policies becomes impossible in a lawless society.

No regime in a divided South Africa will be able to afford commercial pesticides. Its leaders will be vulnerable to the blandishments of foreign entrepreneurs and aid agencies wishing to off-load dangerous pesticides onto them. Several African countries have already fallen prey to European nations seeking a far-off dumping ground for toxic and other hazardous wastes. Access to millions of dollars in hard currency for the sake of a few thousand tonnes of First World garbage will be a temptation too great to resist. For a while at least, South Africa could become the world's favourite dumping ground for hazardous wastes.

Geological exploration will be stopped by companies because of the danger of sending geologists into the bush. Standards of safety on the mines will gradually fall, as senior mining staff and engineers leave the country. Labour unrest and strikes will increase in the short term, quickening the close-down of mining operations when they cease to be viable.

Government may ineffectually step into a direct management role to try to avert the decline of the mining industry. Factories in small towns will ultimately be abandoned in full working order, as managers and workers flee to the safety of the big cities.

Disappearance of nature reserves

The existing network of nature reserves will collapse, not necessarily because of public apathy. The reasons will rather be the breakdown of infrastructure and vehicles, and the lack of spares and fuel supplies. Staff will no longer be trained and plans to maintain a continuity of skills will fall away. The potential gains to be made from wildlife and tourism will be lost. Neither foreign nor local tourists will risk visiting national parks vulnerable to guerrilla activity. The numbers of visitors to Quicama and Gorongoza National Parks in Angola and Mozambique dropped by 90% within a month of the start of civil war in these countries. Both parks – among the most spectacular in Africa – have been closed for many years.

The absence of supplies of Western medicines and pharmaceuticals will raise the exploitation of indigenous 'muti' plants and animals, possibly driving some species to extinction. The muti trade is already a multi-million rand business in South Africa. As many as eight out of every ten Sowetan residents use traditional medicines in preference to modern pharmaceuticals, despite the city's sophisticated medical infrastructure which has a higher doctor-to-patient ratio than any state in black Africa.

Marine resources, especially the west coast fisheries, will become even more vulnerable to foreign marauders. Dumping of toxic wastes at sea may occur, either with the blessing of corrupt officials or because of the absence of law enforcement.

Our 'world in one country' will be reduced to a desolate wasteland. Our paradise – the jewel in the African crown – will be lost.

'SEPARATE IMPOVERISHMENT': LIFE ON THE 'LOW ROAD'

Fortress under siege

The 'Low Road' implies the continuation of 'Grand Apartheid': white rule over the bulk of South Africa with no major change to the present homeland boundaries. The country will become increasingly isolated and, as unrest intensifies, it will take on the appearance of a fortress under siege.

'SEPARATE IMPOVERISHMENT'

✳ **A fortress under siege**
✳ **Continued partition, full restoration of Group Areas Act**
✳ **Mandatory sanctions, disinvestment**
✳ **Centralized, controlled economy**
✳ **Economic downturn, unemployment**
✳ **2% per year or lower GDP growth**
✳ **Larger agricultural subsidies, increased farming debt**
✳ **Political instability, repressive legislation**
✳ **Inadequate financing and staffing for environmental management**

Chart 44

Neither finances nor public commitment will permit more than weak, understaffed and ineffective environmental management activities. Some wildlife areas, such as the Kruger National Park, will survive, jealously protected by paramilitary staff more concerned with their own survival than with that of the animals and plants under their protection.

The First and Third World economies of South Africa will be kept segregated. Thus, the bulk of the black community's income will be devoted to basic needs, such as grain foods, fuel, transport and rented accommodation. Their inability to afford luxury items such as meat, appliances and clothing will slow growth in these industries.

The white community will increase spending on personal security, insurance and pension funds. A plunging rand will cause a major downturn in demand for imported goods. New cars will be several times as expensive as houses.

The partitioning of South Africa into black and white states will be maintained. Further homelands – KwaNdebele, Lebowa and Kwa-Zulu – will be forced into 'independence'. Increased efforts to develop commercial farming enterprises as large economic units in the homelands will widen the chasm between landowners and the landless. Agricultural productivity will decrease. The re-enforcement of homeland policies will once again uplift the status of traditional tribal authorities despite an appreciable desire to move away from tribalism.

Partition will require the return of influx control, and the complete restoration and rigorous enforcement of the Group Areas Act. Spatial separation of dormitory cities from the workplace will persist. Inadequate housing, transportation, schooling, employment and infrastructure for blacks is a feature of this scenario. Squatter settlements will grow despite their illegality, while the level of abject poverty, currently at over 40% in some TBVC states, will increase. White housing needs will be met by increased subsidies in the public and private sectors. However, as affluence declines with the economic downturn, so the value of subsidies will be offset by increased taxation.

Ultimately, the 'Low Road' will reduce South Africa to a state segregated into a relatively affluent, but insecure, ageing, intellectually impoverished and isolated white minority; and a large, youthful, aggressive and economically deprived black majority. The 'Low

Road' will prevent the black population from progressing through the demographic transition to moderate population growth. It will force greater and greater numbers into the destitution of rural and urban slums.

The demands of keeping a minority regime in power, together with maintaining a tightly controlled economy, will displace all other considerations. Certainly, an equitable quality of life and environmental health for all South Africans will be given short shrift. Meanwhile, the sun will slowly but surely set on the Verwoerdian ideal, as the dream of apartheid turns into the nightmare of missed opportunities.

As in 'Paradise Lost', a slowed national economy will reduce the pressure of the industrial, mining and agricultural sectors on natural resources. The condition of our deteriorating rangelands will improve in some areas. Similarly, the rate at which land is transformed from natural vegetation into industrial parks and infrastructure will be reversed. The loss of export markets for maize, sugar, fruit, wool, mohair and other agricultural products due to sanctions will halt the development of cropland and bring down stock numbers. But measured against the negative economic impacts of the 'Low Road', these advantages will be trivial.

Back to socialism and welfare

A 'Low Road' economy will place tremendous pressures on the resources of both white and black rural areas through overpopulation. The rapidly expanding urban squatter camps that develop regardless of laws or regulations during the next decade will exhaust the resource base around the towns as well.

The struggle to survive in a failing economy will savagely deplete the amount of public and private funds spent on environmental conservation. In addition, South Africa's political isolation will mean the curtailment of any foreign aid. South Africa's recent advances in the field of nature conservation will slide backwards by half a century as game rangers return to armed horseback patrols in order to combat poaching.

The government will prop up white commercial farming by maintaining strict controls in the agricultural economy. Subsidies will be boosted for drought relief, and state initiatives on soil conservation will intensify. More support for white farmers in the border areas will be provided. At the last count, state aid to white farmers contributed 20% of net farming income: 58% of the aid went to price stabilization, 15% to fuel rebates, 13% to soil conservation and water provision, and 10% to fertilizer subsidies. For all that, the commercial farming sector has a massive R14 000 million debt, rangeland is declining in potential, and whites continue to leave the rural areas. Not even substantial government hand-outs can halt the exodus.

Under 'Separate Impoverishment', a farming community emerges

ENVIRONMENTAL CONSEQUENCES OF 'SEPARATE IMPOVERISHMENT'

Positive
* Collapse of some agricultural exports (mohair, wool) assists veld recovery
* Slowdown in economy reduces pressure on some resources

Negative
* Overstocking of rangeland
* Crop farming on marginal land
* Subsidized mismanagement of agriculture
* Soil erosion, especially in overpopulated homelands
* Use of cheaper, locally-produced persistent pesticides
* Failure of homeland agriculture
* Widespread deforestation for fuel wood
* Use of low-quality coal in urban areas
* Inadequate provision of water
* Increased health risks
* National parks vulnerable to surrounding populations who are alienated
* Uncontrolled infestation by alien plants

Chart 45

which is neither innovative nor self-supporting. Low returns on capital investment will flow from farmers' short-term planning horizons. By introducing new cropping and livestock schemes with a quick payback, they will gamble with the weather in a futile attempt to erase debts. The intervention of control boards may lead to a 'yo-yo' profile of exaggerated over- and undersupply of produce.

The level of pesticide use will primarily be determined by direct cost, the issue of environmental impact being overshadowed by the need to support the white agricultural economy. Imported pesticides will be too expensive, and farmers will move to cheaper, locally manufactured, but more persistent pesticides. Not only the target pests will be eradicated: a wide spectrum of nontarget animals, plants and humans will also be affected.

South Africa will lose much of its scientific manpower to emigration as the siege economy is prolonged. With the departure of these specialists will go the capacity to implement advanced biotechnological systems. Opportunities to increase agricultural and pharmaceutical production, and to improve waste treatment and pollution control, will have to be passed up and may never come again. Scientists emigrating from South Africa will not return.

The greatest drain of scientists will be among young graduates entering their most productive years. The loss of a generation or more of potential leaders in science and technology will cripple any attempt to revitalize the national economy even if, by some miracle, a democratic government follows a few decades of 'Separate Impoverishment'.

The quasi-subsistence economy in the homelands will continue to depend on money being sent home by city labourers. Migratory labour will be perpetuated, disrupting families and the quality of life. The rising population density will place increased pressure on homeland resources. A poverty-stricken community will eke out a living, with low aspirations compounded by poor education, the absence or scarcity of property rights and depressed economic investment. Furthermore, agricultural 'betterment' schemes in the homelands sponsored by the central government will fail, as the villagers reject the autocratic, top-down management style of the bureaucracy.

Agricultural production in white farming areas will keep on supporting black food needs as far as possible. But the ever increasing number of mouths to feed will eventually push production from arable and grazing land well beyond sustainable limits.

South Africa's abundant resources of low-cost coal will continue to be the country's main energy source. The use of coal- and wood-burning stoves in black urban areas will raise the levels of pollution above health-damaging thresholds for at least part of the year. The country's increased dependence on coal-based liquid fuel resources will necessitate the expansion of existing Sasol facilities. This, in the short term, will lead to even more emissions. However, in the long run, the total volume of emissions will stabilize as lack of foreign investment hampers further development of major power stations. Without adequate urban electrification, mass education programmes and social upliftment for the many millions of urban blacks – through the medium of television – become impossible.

Fuel wood will remain the primary source of energy for rural black populations. Woodlots are unlikely to expand at the required rate on account of resistance from the black population to centrally planned schemes. A transition from fuel wood to cattle dung as an energy source will take place in areas where the woody vegetation has disappeared. The homelands' energy economy will resemble that of parts of India, where the woody vegetation cover has been lost, leaving the soil unprotected. Potential soil-building nutrients, instead of being recycled through cattle dung, will go up in smoke. The scene will be set for the total collapse of soil resources.

The Lesotho Highlands Water Project may compensate, in the short term, for the major geographical mismatch between water availability and need. But this project is vulnerable if the political climate in the region is volatile. More importantly, it cannot mitigate the appalling water shortages to which the impoverished majority is subjected in many areas.

It is unlikely that the government will reduce subsidies on the supply of irrigation water to white farmers. This will exacerbate the problem of making water available to industry and urban areas. Major capital projects to upgrade water supply will probably be delayed or cancelled through lack of finance. A crisis will occur in the early 21st century in terms of both quality and quantity of water.

The socioeconomic impact of a water crisis will be magnified by the interdependence of water, energy and the economy. A Chamber of Mines study estimated that a 20% drop in electricity supply for three months, due to a water shortage, would incur a loss of more than R400 million in foreign exchange and R150 million in taxes. About 38 000 people would be made temporarily or permanently redundant.

The existing network of nature reserves will become increasingly vulnerable to poaching, veld fires and illegal extraction of indigenous medicinal plants as these areas become isolated within each partitioned state. Although it is improbable that any species will become extinct as a consequence, many will be recategorized on the list of threatened species from 'vulnerable' to 'endangered'. Indigenous forest patches will be particularly at risk in the homelands, where growing human numbers and declining law enforcement will result in rapid deforestation. A lack of funds for the control of alien plants will lead to an invasion of woody weeds, with the exception of areas where they will be inadvertently controlled through their exploitation for fuel wood.

The 'Low Road' will perpetuate the South African partitionists' dream of separate but equal states for each ethnic group. But instead of sharing in the country's wealth, the only commodity to be shared will be impoverishment – equally and separately.

A NEW SOUTH AFRICA: TAKING THE 'HIGH ROAD'
Before describing the last two scenarios, which are predicated on the 'High Road', we shall draw attention to certain features common to both of them. Each scenario illustrates the other South African dream – a holistic one shared by many of its citizens. The dream is of an undivided country where the future is shared by all South Africans, regardless of colour or creed. This dream will not become a reality through sanctions or through the barrel of a gun. It will only be attained through high economic growth which over a period of 10 to 20 years leads to a transformation of society.

The issue of land
The present system of land tenure and allocation will be replaced by one more orientated to free enterprise, in accordance with the philosophy of the 'High Road'. The first step will be the gradual introduction

THE 'HIGH ROAD': A NEW SOUTH AFRICA

* **A phased-in open market system for land tenure**
* **Tax on agricultural land, not on farming profits**
* **Adequate funding and expertise for environmental management**
* **Mandatory homelands policy will go**
* **Increased disposable income for blacks**

Chart 46

of a land tax – based on market values – on all freehold agricultural land. Taxation of profits earned from sales of agricultural produce must simultaneously be reduced. This combined action should stimulate the sale of large areas of poorly managed farmland to more competent farmers, and the rehabilitation of farmland through improved land management practices.

The second step will be the redistribution of land. This does not imply the arbitrary transfer of land from the haves to the have-nots, but rather the provision of equal opportunity to anybody to acquire land, regardless of race, at market prices. Black and white farmers will also have equal opportunities to obtain financial credit, and will have equal access to the advisory services necessary to develop newly available land.

Access to land for small market gardens and subsistence farms in peri-urban areas will no longer be for whites only. This land will add yet another vibrant component to the informal sector of the economy.

The current imbalance between white and black incomes will make it necessary to have a phased transition to completely open access to all land. Black farmers initially must be protected by a moratorium on the purchase of land by whites in traditionally black areas. Exceptions could be made for vacant land. If full reciprocity is immediately granted, with blacks being permitted to buy anywhere in white areas and vice versa, it could lead to vast tracts of the homelands being purchased by white farmers, as well as by foreign and local companies, at the inception of the new arrangement.

Free-marketeers might welcome this approach, by arguing that it would lead to an immediate improvement in farming efficiency in the homelands. But the social costs would be excessive. Moreover, the simple transfer of free-market principles from the white agricultural economy to that of black rural areas will almost certainly fail. Land reform in the latter areas will require very careful consideration of the wide diversity of social and cultural conditions that have existed there for centuries. The kind of tenure varies widely from cash crop to pastoral systems and from one geographic area to another.

Decisions to change traditional practices of land tenure must in the end be taken by the communities themselves – a bottom-up rather than a top-down approach to the problem. Ultimately, however, the goal should be a fully fledged free-market system, but this may only come about well into the 21st century.

It is important to note that these moves will not resolve the situation of overcrowding in the homelands, as few black farmers can afford to purchase white farms at the moment. Some will form voluntary cooperatives or companies to do so, but the majority of the inhabitants of the homelands must find other occupations. High economic growth, freedom of movement into and out of urban areas and deregulation of the economy to allow the development of micro-businesses will go a long way towards reducing the pressure of population in black rural areas.

The bottom line is that the mandatory imposition of a homelands policy, with its inordinate social, economic and ecological costs, will have to go in order to make the 'High Road' possible.

The effects of rising black affluence

Increased personal disposable incomes in the black community will allow more general spending on luxury items such as home furnishings and appliances, meat, fruit, clothing, footwear and private transport. This spending will be a major stimulus to the secondary sector of the formal economy, and also to a wide spectrum of activities in the informal sector. The purchase of homes together with investments in insurance and pension funds will further augment the economy.

Higher incomes in the black community will eventually lead to greater spending on recreation, entertainment and holidays. Facilities for mass tourism will expand. Theatres, cinemas and private wildlife parks will be growth businesses. Under the 'High Road' the standard of living of the white population will also improve, though not as spectacularly as that of black consumers.

The 'High Road', therefore, sets new horizons for all South Africans. Political reform, economic growth, education for all, slower population growth – all these suggest an imminent Utopia. But the environmental consequences and sustainability of this Utopia will differ very greatly, depending on how the nation approaches the management of its natural resources – air, water, soil, minerals, plants and animals. We can either go for maximum wealth in the short term, or sustained wealth which can be handed on to future generations. We will now examine the options.

'Boom and Bust': the 'High Road' with no concern for the environment
An internationally acceptable political settlement in South Africa will precipitate a huge economic upswing. The removal of sanctions, foreign investment, the opening of trade with African states, improved socioeconomic standards, education and a new, positive work ethic are sure to contribute to South Africa achieving the status of a newly industrialized country early in the 21st century. We can follow in the footsteps of South Korea, Taiwan, Singapore, Hong Kong and Thailand.

But the GDP growth rate of 5-10% per annum, which a 'High Road' scenario envisages, cannot be achieved without drawing heavily on our natural resources. Thus, in trying to meet the aspirations and expectations that go with a new South Africa, political leaders and the captains of industry will be sorely tempted to forego the constraints that long-term environmental health demands. They will argue persuasively that without the short term, there can be no long term.

The economy will be stimulated by a smaller government and deregulation. Numerous success stories, both from within South Africa and from abroad, show how deregulation has fueled otherwise stagnant economies. We have talked of the enormous growth and multiplier effect of the black taxi industry which is our popular, home-grown model. South Africa, with its history of stifling national legislation and municipal regulations, offers fertile ground for the proliferation of free enterprise as the bureaucratic shackles to economic growth are loosened.

However, concealed within a new economic deal lies a grave danger: the seductive concept that the environmental costs of today's activities can be transferred to the next generation. Play now, pay later.

The *laissez-faire* philosophy of a weak environmental management approach will release many currently restricted areas for private

---

ENVIRONMENTAL CONSEQUENCES OF 'BOOM AND BUST'

Positive
* None

Negative
* Relaxation or abolition of pollution controls leads to massive industrial pollution
* Increased eutrophication and mineralization of water resources
* Agricultural developments destroy remnant forests, river banks, wetlands
* Increased soil erosion, sedimentation
* Indiscriminate use of persistent agricultural pesticides
* Real estate development on sensitive coastal dunes, estuaries, mountain landscapes
* Increased levels of acid rain from power stations burning poor-quality coal
* Withdrawal from international resource conservation convention, e.g. CITES
* Uncontrolled exploitation of rare animals and plants
* Uncontrolled development of tourist and other recreation facilities in privatized national parks and reserves

---

Chart 47

ownership. Minerals, air, water, soil, plants and animals will all be 'fair game' – available to all who wish to compete for their use. Environmental management standards, relating to pollution, soil erosion and wildlife protection, will be relaxed or removed. Market forces will determine the value of each asset, and the profit motive will determine whether the current owner conserves or overexploits the resource.

It cannot be denied that South Africa's maze of legislation needs radical change. Moreover, much of the economic surge of the 'High Road' can occur without controls on resource use and without environmental costs. But many systems are extremely vulnerable and might be irreversibly damaged, with a decline in the quality of life for present and future generations. Let us consider a few cases.

The coastal zone – beaches, intertidal marine communities, estuaries and dune cordons – embraces some of the most vulnerable but sought-after real estate in South Africa. Yet, ironically, the most highly prized qualities of these environments will be eroded, if not destroyed, by uncontrolled access to and use of this zone.

Demand for coastal recreational facilities will double every five years under a 'High Road' economy. To date, however, there is no clear understanding of the effects of development on these sensitive areas. Removal of the present constraints on development within the 1 000 metre coastal zone will almost certainly trigger speculative and destructive exploitation of these finite and very sensitive resources.

Rapid industrial development brings with it a substantial and often unwanted by-product – waste. South Africa currently produces almost 300 million tonnes of solid wastes per annum. Mining wastes contribute 74% of this, with fuel ash from power stations (9%), metallurgical slags (7%) and municipal wastes (6%) accounting for most of the balance.

Although more than 450 mine dumps, encompassing over 3 000 million tonnes of material, already occupy over 10 000 hectares of South Africa, their environmental impact is trivial when measured against the mining industry's contribution to GDP and foreign exchange. But the current management systems, which aim at reducing environmental costs, are expensive and often inadequate. If the mining industry were not compelled to care for the environment, major long-term and irreversible hazards could be encountered.

Relaxed environmental controls will also encourage a move away from the recycling of urban wastes. Currently 460 000 tonnes of waste paper are recycled (30% of the total paper consumption), and 90 000 tonnes, or 15%, of the glass processed come from recycled material. The absence of incentives for recycling will increase the littering problem and ultimately add to the costs of municipal waste removal and disposal systems.

More important than mining or urban wastes, however, are the problems associated with the disposal of hazardous wastes – wastes that have an inherent potential to endanger human, animal or plant life. These are generated by major industries such as chemical, petroleum, metallurgical and manufacturing operations. Inadequate provision for the treatment and disposal of toxic wastes is now costing First World countries billions of dollars annually. Many newly industrialized countries have only recently become aware of the long-term impacts of careless environmental controls during the formative years of their economies. They are now confronted with multibillion dollar clean-up operations.

Because of the high cost of treating and reducing the volume of hazardous wastes, industrialists will be tempted to dispose of these wastes in rivers, landfills or the ocean. Acute short-term, and chronic long-term, environmental damage would occur.

Even nontoxic wastes, such as phosphates and low concentrations of nitrates, can cause major environmental problems through nutrient enrichment – eutrophication – of inland water bodies. Algal blooms and aquatic weeds, such as appeared in the 1970s and early 1980s in the Hartbeespoort dam, have cost millions of rands to control.

In the mid-1980s, legislation was introduced to reduce the quantity of phosphates released in certain catchments by industry, and particularly by municipal sewage works. The legislation appears to have been effective. But even at the relatively low cost of such measures, industry and municipalities would prefer to have the burden of pollution control measures transferred to the next generation, rather than increase this burden for themselves. In some cases, therefore, pollution control legislation is a necessary evil.

South Africa on the 'High Road' will need more electricity. Present networks will have to be expanded and the capacity increased. In the longer term, a transfer from coal-based to nuclear sources is desirable, but for the next few decades our cheap coal will remain the major source of primary energy. The threat of acid rain in the eastern Transvaal Highveld has already been described. In the short term, the costs of reducing emission levels might be unacceptable, but in the long term both the power generating industry and the individual taxpayer will have to carry the cost.

Legislation relating to the protection of the veld and soil resources has existed for over 40 years, but has failed to reduce the negative impacts of overgrazing and soil erosion in all but restricted areas. The expected demand for red meat in a 'High Road' economy will place greatly increased pressure on rangelands. The popular slogan that 'it pays to overgraze' makes economic sense in the short term, but this philosophy will devastate the Karoo, the grasslands and bushveld as we move from the moist 1990s to the arid early years of the 21st century.

Crop farmers, also inspired by higher demand for cereal crops for export to other contries in Africa, will increase their use of pesticides and herbicides, unencumbered by safety regulations either for their workers or for nontarget species.

Wildlife for export, especially endangered species, will earn quick but short-lived profits. The exploitation of the succulent flora of Namaqualand – extremely valued in North America and Western Europe – would provide a temporary windfall for a farming community which has long struggled against an unforgiving climate.

In these circumstances, South Africa may find it expedient to withdraw from international nature conservation conventions, such as the Convention on the International Trade in Endangered Species (CITES). This would provide a bonanza for trade in ivory and rhinoceros horn. If current bans are ineffective and free commerce in these commodities continues, it will be the death knell for the elephant and rhinoceros, whose last refuge in Africa may one day be conservation-conscious southern Africa. The population of African elephants has dropped from an estimated 1,3 million to 625 000 in the last ten years, while the black rhinoceros population has plunged from 65 000 in 1970 to 14 500 in 1980 and 3 500 in 1989.

Thus, 'Boom and Bust' – the golden era of a 'High Road' with weak environmental management policies – will bring great wealth to the individuals who live during the boom. The exploitation of natural resources could make the boom last for decades. But the lessons learnt in most of the older industrialized countries, and all the newly industrialized countries, must ultimately be learnt by South Africa too. The boom will most assuredly be followed by an economic, ecological and quality-of-life bust.

'Rich Heritage': the 'High Road' with a balanced outlook

Under this scenario, a robust economy and a politically stable community will provide the means and the commitment required for the wise use of natural resources. The increased demand for consumer items will call for higher production levels and place certain resources such as water, energy, arable land and grazing lands under pressure.

Under 'Rich Heritage' the risks of reckless resource use through a deregulated economy will be well understood by the nation. Pressure on resources will be reduced by more efficient resource management systems and technologies. A first step will be for government in conjunction with the private sector to reassess land-use potential and practices. By withdrawing marginal land from conventional production, the nation will lay the foundation for the blossoming of a privatized wildlife resource industry.

Vast areas of the USA, Australia and Western Europe are excluded from agricultural use for the simple reason that they are too fragile or unproductive to permit profitable agriculture. But they are ideally suited to outdoor recreation. Similar conditions exist in many areas of South Africa, especially the arid north-west and the mountainous region of the Cape Fold Belt, which should never have been made available for conventional farming.

Although the homelands need many years to recover from the environmental costs of overpopulation and apartheid, an agricultural sector based on a free-market philosophy will gradually emerge. The dismantling of communal ownership and the transition to freehold rights – where this can be implemented with the community's consent – will create an incentive to care for resources. But the concept must be properly promoted. Much of the traditional knowledge and understanding of the environment, which previous generations of

---

ENVIRONMENTAL CONSEQUENCES OF 'RICH HERITAGE'

Positive
* Rehabilitation of degraded marginal lands
* Reduced pressure on homelands
* Growth of privatized wildlife economy
* Electrification of townships
* Development of woodlots
* Improved technologies increase resource life
* Beneficiation adds value to mineral exports
* Increased revenue from outdoor recreation supports expansion of national parks system
* Reduction in livestock population
* Reduced demand for agricultural land through increased productivity
* Integrated pest control
* Application of biotechnology

Negative
* Increased acid rain

Chart 48

black people possessed, has not been passed on to the current generation, many of whom are alienated from the land.

Increased food yields in the homelands will be attained with the establishment of commercial, entrepreneurial farmers on viable landholdings. Private sector initiatives such as the 'Small Farmer Support Systems' can assist with financing. Backyard farming by the urban squatters and rural dwellers will be encouraged. Improved advisory and support services to small farmers and better marketing facilities for livestock should lead to a reduction in herd size and less pressure on the veld.

Rising prosperity, access to decent education and a higher standard of living will foster stable family units in the homelands and create a favourable climate for technology transfer – so vital for the success of 'agricultural upliftment' schemes.

Within white commercial farming, a strong free-market orientation will include the critical review and ultimate withdrawal of all state subsidies and the abolition of central control boards. Private marketing agencies will compete with one another to sell the farmers' produce.

Competitive displacement of incompetent farmers may lead to some rural depopulation. But a dynamic rural community will over time spawn more rural industry and thus increase the population of rural villages. Under 'Rich Heritage', it will be in the interest of landowners to care for their agricultural resources. By doing so they will simultaneously make profits and retain, or improve, the market value of their land. A rise in efficiency of the farming industry brings with it environmental benefits, because rich and successful farmers are among the most effective conservationists.

A substantial jump in demand for red meat from an upwardly mobile black population is expected. But improved animal husbandry, achieving a calving percentage of 60-80% and a livestock 'turnover' rate of 40%, will reduce the required increase in the cattle herd from the present 8 million to only 9,6 million by the year 2000. By contrast, the projected requirement with no change is 12 million head.

A 'Rich Heritage' agricultural economy will allow the raising of animal stocking rates by more intense use of pastures and radical changes to their composition – the best way of overcoming veld degradation. Pastures will also play a vital role on marginal land where new livestock enterprises will provide stability to farming systems currently based on maize. The transfer of one million hectares of marginal maize lands to planted pastures, at a subsidized cost of R280 million, was initiated in 1988. The programme is to be phased over five years.

Legume-based pastures could play a major role in meeting South Africa's future goals for domestic livestock production. The potential exists to convert a total of 17 million hectares to such pastures without reducing crop production. Because of the nitrogen-fixing ability of legumes, it is estimated that such pastures will add over 400 000 tonnes of nitrogen to the soil each year – equivalent to the total amount of artificial nitrogen fertilizer currently used in South Africa.

Higher agricultural production will mean an increased application of pesticides and other chemicals. But a robust economy can afford more expensive and less dangerous types. Moreover, agricultural research organizations will reduce the level of insecticide use by formulating integrated systems of pest control.

Major advances in biotechnology cannot be discounted within the next decade. South Africa's chances of being able to reap the benefits of overseas research will be greatly enhanced through a vigorous local scientific community with active international contacts. It is estimated that R12 000 million is being spent annually in the USA, Western Europe and Japan on research and development in biotechnology. At the University of Cape Town, a biotechnology unit is already working on altering crops to make them more resilient to South African conditions.

Regardless of South Africa's future political dispensation, urbanization is going to be a major environmental issue. But a reasonable solution is only possible with the finances and skills available on the 'High Road'. The experience gained by municipalities, as a result of the more liberal urbanization policies adopted over the past few years, will be invaluable when spending on urban housing is stepped up.

The removal or relaxation of restrictions on small business will stimulate informal-sector activities in the construction industry. By itself, though, the informal sector cannot meet all housing needs. The upgrading of existing squatter settlements and the creation of new ones, the electrification of black urban areas and the development of major new residential areas with the provision of sites and services will only be possible with the utmost cooperation between government, building societies, big business and small black entrepreneurs.

The integration of compact residential areas within and between industrial and commercial sectors will permit the development of 'organic' cities. Distance between home and workplace will be drastically reduced, alleviating the problem of photochemical smog as commuters travel less. Increased productivity will be attained from a work force that does not spend the major portion of its day and night commuting to and from the workplace.

The provision of electricity is a prerequisite for new high-density housing areas. The cost of electrifying 60 existing townships, with a total population of three million, is estimated at just over R700 million in today's terms. But the availability of electricity will stimulate economic development. Small industries will suddenly become a practical possibility; and they will generate a large measure of the revenue needed by Eskom to make the schemes viable.

By relaxing unnecessarily stringent standards, Eskom is already developing cheaper systems of electrical power reticulation. The current cost of R2 500 per house can be reduced to about R1 000. Even with an emphasis on the supply of electricity, woodlots for fuel wood will still be essential for remote rural communities.

In the urban areas, it is not only electricity that has to be universally provided. Adequate road, water and sewage facilities must accompany electrical power reticulation. Without these services, severe aesthetic and environmental health costs will be encountered. Freehold home ownership, better housing, schooling and infrastructure will be followed by a decreasing birth rate and the formation of coherent small family units. With a generally improved quality of life in an attractive rather than a hostile environment, the South African black population will pass through the demographic transition to the same family patterns and life styles as the whites, coloureds and Asians.

Improved living conditions for the black community will rapidly increase water demand for domestic use and for industrial growth. In a country of limited water resources, this has to be offset by more efficient domestic use by the white population and savings in industrial consumption. A 38% reduction in the water used by mines has been achieved in recent years by recycling. Coal-fired power stations have dropped their water consumption by 28%, and the commissioning of dry-cooling in power stations over the next 15 years will reduce water use to a mere 22% of that used in wet-cooled stations. On the domestic front, the drought in Natal in 1984 demonstrated – albeit dramatically – that water consumption could be substantially reduced if necessary.

The greatest water saving could be made by reducing supplies to those irrigation schemes which are most cost-inefficient. Furthermore, domestic water supply in some rural areas could be supplemented by greater *in situ* capture of rainfall.

'Rich Heritage' offers South Africans a unique opportunity. For the first time, a country with extraordinarily plentiful natural resources will have the chance of joining the ranks of newly industrialized countries, with full knowledge of the hazards and costs of imprudent exploitation of those resources. More than this, a new South Africa which is fully accepted in the international community will be able to develop a robust and sustainable economy.

It will be on such an economy that the reconstruction of southern and central Africa can be based. The rich heritage generated by the 'High Road' will benefit not only future generations of South Africans, but future generations to the north as well.

8 Conclusions

Having reached this point in the text, it is hoped that the reader will have come to one conclusion – that the book covers more than the environment. People who expected a standard work on the subject will be surprised at its breadth. At worst they will be disappointed. They may well voice the classic South African complaint: why drag politics into it?

The answer is that life is multidimensional. At the core of sustainable development lies economic growth, the state of the environment and the quality of human life. Each of these three dimensions is essential for the other two to exist. But each does not guarantee the existence of the others. Quite the reverse – going too far in one direction endangers the others. So the three dimensions have to be kept constantly and concurrently in mind.

This book, therefore, has its roots in that all-embracing philosophy of nature whereby the relationship between things matters more than the things in themselves. In any social system, the whole can be greater or less than the sum of its parts, depending on whether there is harmony or discord between them. The Chinese talk of the 'yin' and the 'yang', the Africans speak of 'ubuntu' and a former Prime Minister of South Africa, Jan Smuts, called it 'holism'. A little introspection shows the validity of this outlook: our attitude towards other people is very much influenced by their behaviour towards us, and vice versa. Our relationships can be either constructive or destructive. They determine our intrinsic worth as human beings.

That is why man-made ideologies which simplify life are bound to fail in the end. For example, Marxism advocates collective thinking, apartheid focuses on separateness. Yet we all know that life involves both self-interest and togetherness. Similarly, ideologies which stress these last two qualities to the exclusion of all others are self-defeating. People do possess a social conscience – ethnicity and nationalism are a fact. We cannot disregard any aspect of nature. It is a mixture of opposites, and each of us finds our own balance between them.

One of the great paradoxes of life is that individual liberty taken to the extreme promotes anarchy, but anarchy means no freedom for anyone at all. No wonder that madness is sometimes defined as logical thought carried beyond the bounds of reason!

The second conclusion follows from the first: economic development is crucial for environmental health and quality of life. Without a 20-year period of sustained economic development, there is next to no chance of South Africa reducing the rate at which its population is set to grow. Without a significant drop in population growth there can be little, if any, improvement in the quality of life. Environmental health will worsen as numbers take their toll. Any action which impedes economic growth must, therefore, be highly detrimental to South Africa's future prospects. The action can be imposed on us from outside, in the form of boycotts and sanctions. Or it can be self-inflicted – like the reintroduction of petty apartheid, half-empty teacher training colleges and schools or the needless expense of providing separate government departments and amenities for each population group. The effect is the same: less income, more people.

A rapidly expanding economy is a great healer. That, rather than apartheid, reduces friction between the races. The European Common Market has all but ensured that war will never break out again in Western Europe. There is now too much to lose. Likewise, the chances of conflict here will diminish to virtually zero with the growth of a non-racial business community.

This brings us to the third conclusion, which is the importance of universal access to the country's resources by the population as a whole – whether it be education, health, the economy, minerals or land. It is no good raising average GDP per capita if the incremental gains are confined to a small segment of the population. For a demographic transition to smaller family sizes to occur quickly, the fruits of labour must be spread across all layers of society. But this is not an invitation for the state to intervene to ensure equality of outcome. We want the equality of opportunity which accompanies a free-enterprise system.

The fourth conclusion is the most critical one in the near term both for the world and for South Africa. Trade-offs between economic development, environmental health and quality of life are inevitable. We cannot have our cake and eat it all the time.

For instance, economic growth implies the consumption of more and more electrical energy to improve the quality of human life and to fuel industry. For the foreseeable future, most of this electricity will be coal-generated and common sense, together with the data at our disposal, show that this will, in all likelihood, contribute to the 'greenhouse effect'. Strong economic growth may be sufficient to buy the technology necessary to remove certain pollutants from industries or from cars that burn fossil fuels, but carbon dioxide remains the major pollutant dumped into the atmosphere.

Only the most ardent 'Green' can believe that the problem can be solved by the political leaders of the developed countries advocating a lower standard of living, or by the political leaders of the developing nations arguing for a general use of bicycles. No, the real solution will involve telling people that, in the process of creating wealth, they will have to invest heavily in the following:

- Energy conservation, including more efficient systems and less wastage on unnecessary processes or luxuries.
- The long-term phasing out of fossil fuels, which means the development of alternative and renewable energy sources and safer forms of nuclear energy. For the first time in history, man will have to make do with less of one of his greatest discoveries – fire.
- Waste recovery and disposal technology.

We will soon be obliged to make some sacrifices and changes to our life styles. The cake we eat in 50 years' time will have to be baked in a different way and contain other ingredients.

Caution is, however, called for here. The environment is finite. Technology cannot, for example, make space larger. The model of an environment of limitless resilience is no longer realistic or plausible. The world is simply not large enough to accommodate all the assaults of a rapidly expanding human population and its industries, or a continuation of the industrialists' conventional philosophy of 'focus profits and diffuse costs'.

Thus our call for a free-enterprise economy should not be interpreted as a licence for a freebooting economy. We do not wish anybody to be granted a licence to plunder resources, or to damage the environment and its life-supporting processes indiscriminately. This applies especially to the 'commons', such as the oceans and the atmosphere.

The 'commons' are the world's common resources. Garrett Hardin's essay 'The Tragedy of the Commons' is a modern classic in environmental literature. The 'tragedy', which has 'remorseless inherent logic', is that it is clearly to an individual's advantage to exploit a common resource as thoroughly as possible. Yet if all individuals were to adopt this behaviour, the resource would be exhausted to the detriment of all. Hence, to maintain the world's common resources there must be limitations on the individual's freedom to exploit. "Freedom in a commons," wrote Hardin, "brings ruin to all". Examples of this principle are the collapse of South Africa's west coast pilchard industry and, on a global scale, the decimation of the baleen whale populations. The supreme irony is that just as the world is embracing individualism as an economic philosophy, the state of the environment is demanding collective action.

Accordingly, the fifth conclusion explores the role of government in leading society through the thicket of trade-offs described above. While a free-market system can be an ally for a healthy environment, it can only be so if properly disciplined. If industrialists are left alone and undisciplined in the marketplace, they will regard water and air as free dumping grounds. The discipline in the market must come from government. It is for voters, through their elected government, to decide on the quality of their environment and how much they will pay for its maintenance. The free market cannot do that for them, but the free market can make voters richer, and therefore raise the amount they will be prepared to pay for cleaner air and water.

In essence, the government should provide the rules of the game and then act as coach and referee. But these rules should not be long lists of do's and don'ts, with the government specifying the methods of controlling pollution. Rewards and penalties should be fixed for being better or worse than an affordable set of environmental standards. In effect, air and water should have a price put on them. It should then be left to the market to devise the least expensive means of meeting those standards.

The sixth and last conclusion is that South Africa will need to develop its own shifting balance between the economy, the environment

CONCLUSIONS

* A holistic approach to the environment
* Economic development is paramount, otherwise less income means more people
* Universal access to the country's resources
* Trade-offs are unavoidable
* Government as coach and referee in the environmental game
* No fixed blueprints

but

* Hope for South Africa in attaining 'Rich Heritage'

Chart 49

and the quality of life. Fixed blueprints and rigid prescriptions are not appropriate because they will soon be rendered obsolete by technological developments and changes in the marketplace. Moreover, there are no readily transferable models which have proved successful elsewhere in the world.

Nevertheless, the three of us remain optimistic that South Africans will have the sense to opt for our 'Rich Heritage' scenario – economic development with a strong environmental ethic. But the spirit of entrepreneurship must be liberated. People must also be educated about the importance of safeguarding the interests of future generations by protecting the environment today. Wiping the slate clean of apartheid is one thing: we are fairly confident that this will happen. But what replaces it is even more important. We hope that this book has gone some way towards clarifying the choices. But, in the end, the choice is yours.

Bibliography

During the course of this study, many hundreds of research papers and publications were consulted. The list below includes only those from which statistics or quotations used in the book were drawn.

Acocks, J. P. H. 1975. Veld Types of South Africa. *Memoirs of the Botanical Survey of South Africa.* 40, 1-128.

Adler, E. D. 1985. Soil Conservation in South Africa. Department of Agriculture and Water Supply, Bulletin 406.

Anon. 1985. Basic Needs in Rural Areas. South African National Scientific Programmes Report 116. CSIR, Pretoria.

Anon. 1987. *Our Common Future.* Oxford University Press, Oxford.

Anon. 1987. Abstract of Agricultural Statistics. Department of Agricultural Economics and Marketing, Pretoria.

Anon. 1987. Resources of Southern Africa II. *South African Journal of Science* 83, 246-327.

Brown, L. 1988. *State of the World 1988.* W. W. Norton, New York.

Brunke, E. G. 1988. Tropospheric Background Measurements of $CFCl_3$ (F-11) Conducted at Cape Point, South Africa, since 1979. In: Macdonald, I. A. W. and Crawford, R. J. M. (eds). Long-term Data Series Relating to Southern Africa's Renewable Natural Resources. South African National Scientific Programmes Report 157, 434-435.

Department of Water Affairs 1986. Management of the Water Resources of the Republic of South Africa. Department of Water Affairs, Pretoria.

De Vos, T. J. 1987. Regional Housing Requirements and Affordability in South Africa. NBRI, CSIR, Pretoria.

Loubser, M. 1986. Black Income and Expenditure Patterns: 1985 and 2000. Unpublished MS. Bureau of Market Research, UNISA, Pretoria.

Macdonald, I. A. W. and Crawford, R. J. M. (eds). 1988. Long-term Data Series Relating to Southern Africa's Renewable Natural Resources. South African National Scientific Programmes Report 157.

Myers, N. (ed). 1985. *The Gaia Atlas of Planet Management*. Pan Books, London.

Mostert, W. P. and van Tonder, J. L. 1982. Moontlike Bevolkingsgroei in Suid-Afrika tot die Middel van die 22e Eeu. HSRC, Pretoria.

Pearman, G. I. 1988. Greenhouse Gases: Evidence for Atmospheric Changes and Anthropogenic Causes. In: Pearman G. I. (ed). *Greenhouse: Planning for Climate Change*. CSIRO Publications, Melbourne. pp 3-21.

Pearman, G. I. (ed). 1988. *Greenhouse: Planning for Climate Change*. CSIRO Publications, Melbourne.

Pittock, A. B., Ackerman, T. P., Crutzen, P. J., MacCracken, M. C., Shapiro, C. S. and Turco, R. P. 1985. *Environmental Consequences of Nuclear War*. Volume 1: Physical and Atmospheric Effects. SCOPE 28. John Wiley, Chichester.

Potgieter, J. F. 1988. The Household Subsistence Level in the Major Urban Centres of the Republic of South Africa. Institute for Planning Research, Fact Paper 72, University of Port Elizabeth.

President's Council 1983. Report of the Science Committee of the President's Council on Demographic Trends in South Africa. Government Printer, Pretoria.

Scotney, D. M. 1988. The Agricultural Areas of Southern Africa. In: Macdonald, I. A. W. and Crawford, R. J. M. (eds). Long-term Data Series Relating to Southern Africa's Renewable Natural Resources. South African National Scientific Programmes Report 157, 316-336.

Tyson, P. D. 1987. *Climatic Change and Variability in Southern Africa*. Oxford University Press, Cape Town.

Tyson, P. D., Kruger, F. J. and Louw, C. W. 1988. Atmospheric Pollution and its Implications in the Eastern Transvaal Highveld. South African National Scientific Programmes Report 150, CSIR, Pretoria.

World Resources Institute 1988. *World Resources 1988-89*. Basic Books, New York.